FamilyCircle

CRAFTS FOR CHRISTMAS

EDITORIAL

Editorial Director, Family Circle Books — Carol A. Guasti
Associate Editor — Kim E. Gayton
Project Editor — Leslie Gilbert Elman
Copy Editor — Laura Crocker
Book Design — Bessen, Tully & Lee
Cover Photo — David Bishop
Cover Calligraphy — Anthony Bloch
Clip Art-1,001 Advertising Cuts from the 20's and 30's, copyright© 1987 by Dover Publications, Inc; Ready-To-Use Old Fashioned Christmas Illustrations, copyright© 1989 by Dover Publications, Inc.
Editorial Production Coordinator — Celeste Bantz
Editorial Assistant — Sherieann Holder
Senior Typesetter — Alison Chandler
Typesetting — Maureen Harrington, Cheryl Aden
Indexer — Candace Gylgayton

MARKETING

Director, Family Circle Books & Licensing — Margaret Chan-Yip
Direct Marketing Manager — Jill E. Schiffman
Associate Business Manager — Carrie Meyerhoff
Administrative Assistant — Laura Berkowitz

Published by The Family Circle, Inc.
110 Fifth Avenue, New York, NY 10011

Copyright® 1991 by The Family Circle, Inc.

Manufactured in the United States of America

10 9 8 7 6 5 4 3 2 1

Library of Congress Cataloging in Publication Data
Main entry under title:

Family circle crafts for christmas.
Includes index.

1.Christmas decorations.   2.Christmas crafts.   I.Family Circle, Inc.   II.Title: Crafts For Christmas.
1991   91-065848
ISBN 0-933585-24-1

Other Books By Family Circle

BEST-EVER RECIPES

BEST-EVER RECIPES, VOLUME II

THE BEST OF FAMILY CIRCLE COOKBOOK SERIES
(Pub. Dates: 1985 – 1989)

BUSY COOK'S BOOK

GOOD HEALTH COOKBOOK

MAKE IT COUNTRY

THE COUNTRY KITCHEN

COUNTRY CRAFTS

THE FAMILY CIRCLE CHRISTMAS TREASURY SERIES
(Pub. Dates: 1986 – 1991)

TREASURY OF CHRISTMAS CRAFTS

FAVORITE NEEDLECRAFTS

HINTS, TIPS & SMART ADVICE

To order **FamilyCircle** books, write to Family Circle Books, 110 Fifth Avenue, New York, NY 10011.

To order **FamilyCircle** magazine, write to Family Circle Subscriptions, 110 Fifth Avenue, New York, NY 10011.

TABLE OF CONTENTS

INTRODUCTION 1

WELCOME CHRISTMAS 2
Holiday Door Trims   4
Let There Be Lights   14

YULETIDE TABLE MAGIC 20
Set the Table, Set the Mood   22
Centerpieces and Accents   28
Holiday Table Linens   36

ALL THROUGH THE HOUSE 46
Grand Victoriana   48
A Contemporary Country Christmas   56
Ornaments to Treasure   72

OVERNIGHT SENSATIONS 88
Terrific Trims   90
Gifts in a Flash   98

PRESENTS, PRESENTS, PRESENTS! 104
Gifts for the Home   106
Especially for Her   114
Just for Him   122
The Kids' Corner   134

Crafts Basics and Abbreviations   158
Stitch Guide   168
Index   170
Photographers and Crafts Editors Credits   172

INTRODUCTION

It's the most glorious season of year. A time for celebrating all that is good, generous and loving. A time to gather together with family and special friends, to cherish the joy in your lives and the love you share.

Family Circle has been helping you to "make the season bright" for almost 60 years. This year we welcome Christmas with beautiful door trims and twinkling lights, delightful table settings and wonderful ornaments. Each chapter brings another facet of the Yuletide season into your home. From decorating magnificent trees to adding lovely accents, there's something within these pages that will help make this Christmas especially wonderful.

Because one of the greatest joys of Christmas is giving something to your loved ones, we provide you with gifts for the home, for her, for him, and for those special children in your life. Remember—the greatest gift is the gift of love. And what better way to show your love than by taking the time to hand-craft your Christmas presents.

As always, there are hints to help make crafting decorations and gifts simple and easy. But this year we've also included some very special, ecologically sound "Tips for a Green Christmas" to insure bright holidays for our children and our children's children.

WELCOME CHRISTMAS

Be
merry all,
Be merry all,
With holly dress the festive hall;
Prepare the song,
the feast, the ball,
To welcome merry Christmas.
—W. R. Spencer

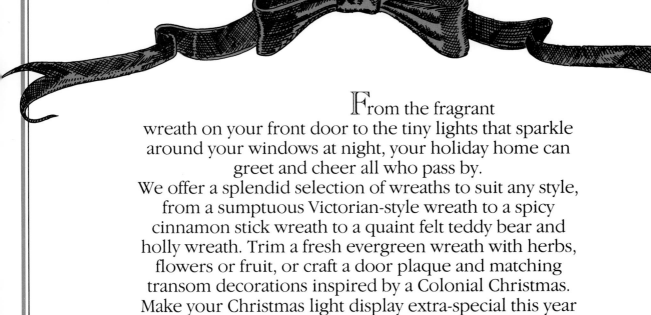

From the fragrant
wreath on your front door to the tiny lights that sparkle
around your windows at night, your holiday home can
greet and cheer all who pass by.
We offer a splendid selection of wreaths to suit any style,
from a sumptuous Victorian-style wreath to a spicy
cinnamon stick wreath to a quaint felt teddy bear and
holly wreath. Trim a fresh evergreen wreath with herbs,
flowers or fruit, or craft a door plaque and matching
transom decorations inspired by a Colonial Christmas.
Make your Christmas light display extra-special this year
with an old-fashioned village scene in your window. Or
create the illusion of stars falling through tree branches.
Let the beauty of your Yuletide home give all who pass
by a greeting of love, peace and welcome.

HOLIDAY DOOR TRIMS

Adorn your front door
and entryway with holiday splendor
to greet the season.

ANTIQUE DOLL WREATH

(photo, page 3 and at left)
This beautiful, Victorian-style wreath may look ornate, but actually it is very easy to make.

Easy: Achievable by anyone.

Materials: Ceramic doll head (available at craft supply and hobby stores); antique-look decals; dried baby's breath; 1¼-inch-wide double-edged ecru lace; 2-inch-wide double-edged ecru lace; ⅛-inch-wide pink, red and green velvet ribbons; 1-inch-wide pink, red and green velvet ribbons; roll of gold metallic wrapping paper; sheets of lightweight poster board; floral foam; floral wire; stapler; glue stick; rubber cement; carbon paper; paper for pattern.

Directions:

1. Trace the full-size cornucopia pattern in FIG. I, 1 *(page 6)* onto paper. Using the carbon paper, trace the pattern onto the poster board 30 times. Repeat on the gold paper. Cut out all the cornucopias. Also draw and cut out a 15-inch-diameter circle from the poster board.

2. Roll each poster board cornucopia into a cone, lapping the edges ¼ inch. Secure the edges with the glue stick, and staple them together along the top edge.

3. Spread rubber cement on the backs of the gold paper cornucopias, and cover each poster board cornucopia with a gold cornucopia. Trim all the gold-covered cornucopias with the ribbons and laces; add the decals to 10 of the cornucopias *(see photo, page 3)*.

4. Fill each cornucopia with floral foam, and insert bunches of baby's breath into the foam.

5. Cover the poster board circle with gold wrapping paper, gluing down the paper edges securely in the back. Glue the 20 cornucopias without decals evenly spaced around the gold circle like the spokes of a wheel. Glue the 10 cornucopias with decals on top of the plain gold cornucopias, placing them between and on top of the first layer *(see photo)*.

6. Gather the ⅛-inch-wide velvet ribbons into loops to make a bow with 30-inch-long streamers, and wire the loops together. Wire the bow and streamers to the center of the wreath *(see photo)*. Wire the doll head to the center of the wreath above the bow.

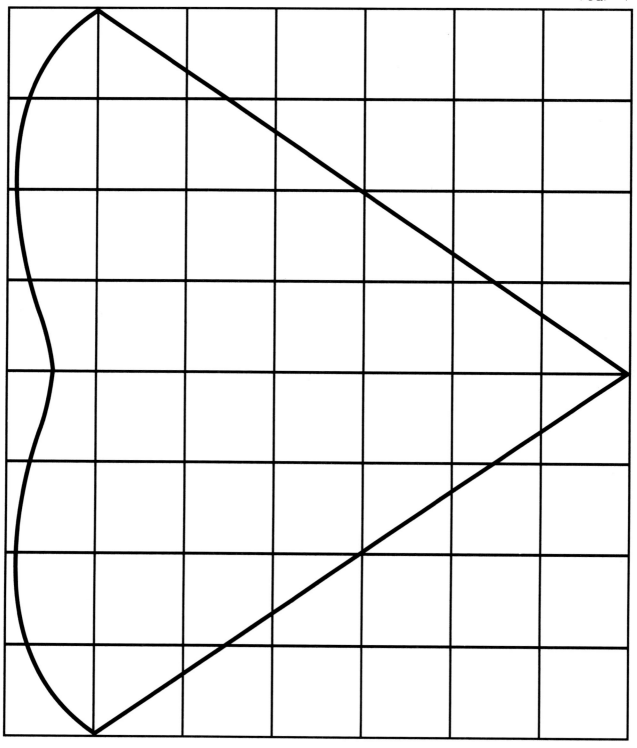

FOLK ART GOOSE

Hang this inviting folk art plaque on the front door to provide a special welcome to holiday guests.

Challenging: Requires more experience in painting.

Materials: 10 x 12 inches of plywood; graphite paper; stylus, or dry ballpoint pen; fine garnet sandpaper; tack cloth; oil paints: titanium white, ivory black, burnt umber, burnt sienna, Prussian blue, cadmium yellow light, cadmium yellow medium, cadmium red pale or light, cadmium red medium, and alizarin crimson; acrylic paints: white and black; clear matte-finish acrylic spray; polyurethane *(optional)*; paintbrushes: No. 2 flat, No. 6 flat, and small round brush or No. 1 liner; 1-inch sponge brush; palette paper; palette knife; odorless mineral spirits; paper toweling; jigsaw or sabre saw; tracing paper for pattern.

Directions:

1. Enlarge the goose pattern in FIG. I, 2 *(page 8)* onto tracing paper, following the directions on page 169. Using the graphite paper and stylus or dry ballpoint pen, trace the goose shape onto the plywood. Cut out the goose shape, and sand the edges smooth. Remove all the sawdust with the tack cloth.

2. Stain the back of the goose with burnt umber oil paint thinned with mineral spirits. Let the stain dry for 30 minutes.

3. Using the sponge brush, apply a coat of white acrylic paint to the front of the goose. Let the paint dry for 15 minutes. Sand the paint lightly, and remove all the sawdust with the tack cloth. Apply a second coat of white paint. Let the paint dry thoroughly.

4. Using the graphite paper and stylus or dry ballpoint pen, trace the detail lines onto the painted goose front.

5. Using the round or liner brush and black acrylic paint, paint the eye oval and eyelashes. Let the paint dry. Mist the eye with the clear acrylic to seal it.

6. Use the oil paints as they come from the tube; use only enough paint to cover an area. To clean the brushes between colors, wipe them well with paper toweling; do not use mineral spirits on the brushes while painting. Mix a soft bluish, blackish-gray using Prussian blue, a small amount of ivory black and a very small amount of titanium white. Shade around the eye, under the cheek, the wing, and the feathers with a dry No. 2 flat brush; apply a small amount of gray, and stretch it to cover. Soften the shading with the No. 6 flat brush to create a shadow effect; the darkest area should be where the holly shades the body. Mist the shading with the clear acrylic spray to seal it. Add a dot of titanium white to highlight the eye.

FIG. I, 2 FOLK ART GOOSE   1 SQ. = 1″

W = WHITE   B = BLACK   Y = YELLOW   R = RED   G = GREEN

7. Using the No. 2 flat brush, paint the beak cadmium yellow medium. Pat on a touch of cadmium red pale or light to shade the beak where it joins the head, and at the division between the upper and lower beak. Tone with a touch of burnt sienna, if necessary. Highlight the division with titanium white. Using the round brush, paint the nostril ivory black.

8. Mix a medium dark green using cadmium yellow light and a small amount of ivory black. Use the dark green on the leaf vein lines, and where one leaf overlaps another. Add just a little Prussian blue to the dark green on the palette paper to brighten the color. Apply the brighter green around the outside edges of the leaves, letting the background show through as a highlight. Paint the berries with the round brush, using cadmium red medium as the basic color. Using burnt sienna, paint the holly stems with rather broken lines to look like branches.

9. Paint the letters with the small round or No. 2 flat brush and the gray paint used for the shading; thin the paint with one or two drops of mineral spirits. Make the edges of the letters clean and crisp.

10. Mist the painted goose very carefully and lightly with the clear acrylic spray, holding the can at least 12 inches away from the plaque and keeping the can moving continuously. If the clear acrylic is applied too heavily, it will crack and craze the paint. Mist the goose two or three times, letting the acrylic dry between coats. The acrylic spray finish is sufficient protection if the plaque is hung indoors, or in a protected outdoor area. If you wish to hang the plaque in an unprotected outdoor area, apply two or three coats of polyurethane to both sides of the plaque, sanding lightly between coats.

CLEVER CRAFTING

Forever Flowers

Yarrow, statice and baby's breath, the flowers called for in the Field of Flowers Wreath at right, all can be air dried. Air drying is the easiest way to dry fresh flowers.

● Tie six to ten stems together with string or a rubber band. Hang the bunches of flowers upside down in a dark, dry spot where air circulates freely — an attic, spare room, shady kitchen corner, or closet with the door left open a crack. Flowers dried in the dark last longer and maintain a truer color.

● The dried stems of some flowers, such as strawflowers and globe amaranth, are too brittle to work well, so replace them with wire before drying the flower heads. Pinch off each stem close to the bottom of the fresh bud or flower. Push a length of 16-gauge wire midway into the flower head. Place the flowers upright in a container. As they dry, the flowers will open and adhere to the wires.

● Most flowers will air dry in two to three weeks unless the weather is very humid.

● Leave bunches of air dried flowers hanging until you are ready to use them, or untie and store them, loosely packed, in a covered box.

● Some flowers, such as annual and perennial statice, baby's breath, yarrow, strawflowers, hydrangea, globe amaranth and oregano blossoms, can be dried upright; simply place them in a vase. Be sure to strip the leaves from yarrow after picking it.

FIELD OF FLOWERS WREATH

Trim a traditional evergreen wreath with summer's glory.

Easy: Achievable by anyone.

Materials: Pine or other evergreen wreath; fresh or dried flowers: golden yarrow, blue statice and baby's breath; floral wire.

Directions:
Attach short lengths of floral wire to the yarrow and statice about 2 inches below the flower heads. Trim the stems slightly below the wires so that when the flower heads are wired to the wreath, they will sit on the wreath with nothing of the stems showing through. Wire the yarrow to the wreath. Fill in with the statice. Tuck in the baby's breath as accents.

CLEVER CRAFTING

Sap Solution

Here's a quick way to remove pine cone "sap" from your hands: Put a few drops of vegetable oil on your hands, rub briskly then wash with soap and water.

CINNAMON STICK WREATH

Easy: Achievable by anyone.

Materials: Plywood or corrugated cardboard ring; several dozen cinnamon sticks; white glue; ¾ yard of 3-inch-wide velvet ribbon; dried or artificial flowers, or dried herbs; floral wire.

Directions:
1. Lay the plywood or cardboard ring on a flat surface. Using the photo as a guide, place the cinnamon sticks on top of the ring in a pleasing arrangement.
2. When you are satisfied with the arrangement, glue the sticks to the ring, a section at a time, by spreading glue over the entire width of the ring and replacing the cinnamon sticks on the ring carefully. Let the glue dry.
3. Fold in each end of the velvet ribbon to make two loops that cross in the center *(see photo)*. Hold the loops in place like a bow with a length of floral wire wrapped around the center. Glue some flowers or herbs over the wire to conceal it. Glue the bow over a sparse area of the wreath. Glue extra cinnamon sticks and flowers behind it.
4. Wire the flowers or herbs into small bunches. Evenly space the bunches around the wreath, and glue them in place. Let the glue dry thoroughly before hanging the wreath.

COLONIAL CHRISTMAS ENTRYWAY PLAQUES

Average: For those with some experience in crafting.

Materials: Floral oasis cage (block of oasis surrounded by chicken wire; available at nurseries and garden centers); pine or other evergreen branches; branches of dried white poplar leaves; bayberry, bittersweet or other branches with berries; pine cones; red apples; No. 22 or 24 floral wire; floral picks.

Directions:

1. Wrap a length of floral wire around the base of each pine cone. Wire each apple to a floral pick by cutting two 5-inch lengths of floral wire, and inserting one wire through the apple near the bottom. Insert the second wire at the same level at right angles to the first wire. Pull the four wire ends down, and twist them around a floral pick held against the bottom of the apple; do not puncture the apple with the pick.

2. Using the photo as a design guide, insert the pine or other evergreen branches into the oasis cage to define a pleasing outline for the plaque. Fill in the plaque's shape with the poplar leaf and berry-laden branches. Attach the pine cones and apples to the center of the plaque in a pleasing arrangement.

3. Make the transom decorations following Steps 1 and 2 above, using slightly smaller oasis cages.

TIPS FOR A "GREEN" CHRISTMAS

Apples Twice Over

The apples you use on your wreaths will look beautiful for a couple of weeks, but they'll eventually start to wither. Replace them with new apples to keep your decorations looking fresh. Cut up the old apples (seeds and all) and leave them out for the birds.

Directions:

1. Using the compass, draw a 5½-inch-diameter circle on the cardboard. Draw a 3½-inch-diameter circle inside the first circle to make a small wreath shape. Cut out the cardboard wreath shape with the craft knife. Using the cardboard shape as a pattern, cut out nine more small wreaths from the cardboard.

2. Glue the cardboard wreath shapes together in pairs to make five double-thickness small wreaths.

3. Trace the full-size holly leaf and bear patterns in Figs. I, 3A and 3B onto paper, and cut out the patterns.

4. Cut 80 holly leaves from the green felt. Glue the leaves together in pairs, placing a pipe cleaner between each pair to form a middle rib; let the excess pipe cleaner extend beyond the bottom point of the leaves to form the stem. Let the glue dry completely.

5. Attach eight double holly leaves to each small wreath by gluing their stems to the cardboard. Let the glue dry completely. Bend each leaf where it meets its stem to shape it.

6. Cut 30 green felt holly leaves. Glue six leaves to each small wreath to cover the cardboard and leaf stems completely. Let the glue dry.

HOLLY BEAR WREATH

Easy: Achievable by anyone.

Materials: 9 x 12-inch craft felt rectangles: 20 of green, 5 of old gold, and 1 each of white and black; 2½ yards of 1-inch-wide red ribbon; 1 yard of Red yarn; 41 pipe cleaners; corrugated cardboard; synthetic stuffing; craft knife; black fine-point permanent felt tip pen; small hole paper punch; compass; tacky white craft glue; paper for patterns.

Note: *Five small wreaths are assembled, and attached to form the large wreath.*

FIG. I, 3A HOLLY
BEAR WREATH

FULL SIZE

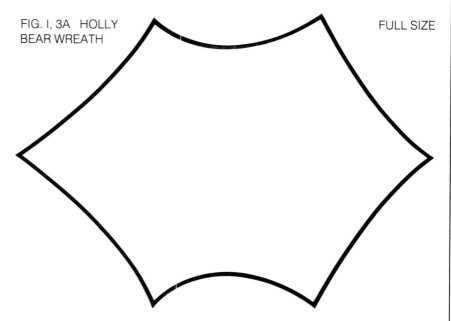

7. Arrange the small wreaths, right side down, in a circle to form a large wreath. Cut out five 5½ x 1½-inch cardboard strips. Apply glue to one cardboard strip and place it, glue side down, on two adjacent small wreaths so that half the strip is on each wreath. Repeat to glue all the small wreaths together. Cut out additional green felt holly leaves, and glue them to the large wreath to cover any visible cardboard.

8. Cut out ten bears from the old gold felt. Glue a pair of bears together as close to the felt edges as possible, leaving an opening for stuffing. Repeat with the remaining bears. Let the glue dry completely. Stuff each double bear lightly, and glue the opening closed.

9. Cut out 30 small white felt circles for the bears' paw pads and inner ears. Cut out five white felt ovals for the bears' stomachs *(see photo)*. Glue the paw pads, inner ears, and stomachs in place. Cut out five 1¼-inch-diameter white felt circles. Cut into each circle's center along a radius, lap one cut edge over the other to form a slight cone shape, and glue the lapped edges together. Place a small amount of stuffing inside each cone, and glue a cone to each bear's face for a muzzle *(see photo)*. Cut out black felt eyes and noses with the paper punch. Using the photo as a placement guide, glue the eyes and noses to the bears. Draw a double curve mouth on each bear with the black felt tip pen. Divide the yarn into five equal lengths, and tie a length around each bear's neck.

10. Using the photo as a placement guide, glue each bear between two small wreaths. Cut five 18-inch lengths of ribbon. Tie each length into a bow, and glue the bow to a small wreath *(see photo)*. Shape the remaining pipe cleaner into a loop, and glue the loop to the back of the large wreath for a hanger.

FIG. I, 3B HOLLY BEAR WREATH   FULL SIZE

13

LET THERE BE LIGHTS

Add a touch of Christmas magic
to your home with sparkling lights
that shine through the winter darkness.

CATCH A FALLING STAR

Average: For those with some experience in crafting.

Materials: Tall, sturdy, bare white birch branches; plastic icicles; strings of white- or green-corded clear, white miniature outdoor lights; strings of clear, white miniature indoor lights *(optional)*; survey stake for each outdoor tree; 2 hose clamps for each outdoor tree; 4 feet of 1 x 2 pine lumber for each indoor tree *(optional)*; 4-inch wood screw for each indoor tree *(optional)*; 1½-inch nails *(optional)*; No. 22 spool wire; wire cutter; saw; screwdriver *(optional)*; hammer *(optional)*.

Directions:

1. Cutting: Cut the birch branches to the desired height.

2. Outdoor Trees: Clamp the top of a survey stake to the bottom of each birch branch to make a "tree." Place the outdoor trees in front and on each side of the window, pushing their stakes firmly into the ground.

3. Indoor Trees (optional): For each indoor tree, cut the 1 x 2 pine lumber into two 18-inch-long legs and two 4-inch-long feet. Nail a foot under each end of one leg, outside edges even. Center the other leg on the upside down footed piece, and use a 4-inch wood screw to attach the legs where they cross. Continue screwing up into the bottom of a branch to make a "tree." Set the indoor trees in front of the window.

4. Attaching Lights: Work with the strings of lights turned on, so you can find the source easily if a problem arises. Starting at the top of each outdoor tree, wire a string of outdoor lights, plug end downward, to a single branch. Follow the shape of the branch closely; do not string the lights from side to side across the branch. Repeat on the other branches. If you are using indoor trees, repeat on them with strings of clear, white miniature indoor lights.

5. Icicles: Wire the plastic icicles into clusters. Wire the clusters to the outdoor trees to create the look of real icicles hanging from the branches *(see photo)*.

WINTER VILLAGE WINDOW SCENE

Easy: Achievable by anyone.

Materials: Electric train set; scale model village with snow-covered trees; white bed sheet; books of varying thicknesses; mirror; strings of clear, white miniature lights; evergreen garlands; several yards of white tulle netting.

Directions:

1. Select a sturdy table that is large enough to hold the train set and village. Place the table in front of the window. Cover the table with the bed sheet, and place the books under the sheet to make plateaus on which to set the village buildings.

2. Assemble the train set, and lay out the village. If the village does not contain lights, you may be able to run a string of lights over the surface of the table, and place a building over each light. Place the mirror in the center of the village as a lake.

3. Drape the garlands around the outside of the window. Twist the light strings around the garlands.

4. Drape the tulle netting over the window's curtain rod so the netting gives the appearance of puffy clouds over the village scene. Run a string of lights behind the netting.

RUSTIC TIN LANTERNS

Make several of these lovely, Mexican-inspired lanterns, and use them to light the front walk when guests are expected. After the party gets started, bring the lanterns indoors as room decorations; don't leave them burning outdoors unattended.

Average: For those with some experience in crafting.

Materials: Coffee, juice, large vegetable or other heavy duty cans; medium-size chunky candles; tin snips; awl; pencil; manila folder *(optional)*; craft knife *(optional)*; silver, red or green spray paint *(optional).*

Directions:

1. Select a cut out design that will let the candlelight shine through, but allows the can to keep its shape; simple slanted line patterns work well. Pencil the design on the can. If the design is fairly complicated, use a craft knife to cut a stencil of the design on a manila folder. Trace the design onto the can with a pencil.

2. Cut out the design on the can with the tin snips, using the awl to make starter holes. Or use the awl to punch out the entire design. When you have finished cutting the design, press down on the top of the can until it bulges slightly *(see photo)*.

3. If you wish, spray paint the lantern.

4. Melt the bottom of the candle slightly, and place the candle so it sits securely on the bottom of the lantern.

TIPS FOR A "GREEN" CHRISTMAS

Outdoor Lights

To help conserve energy, use mini-lights instead of standard-size outdoor Christmas bulbs.

The Light Fantastic

- Set up your display while it's still light outside, then check the effect after dark; you can't get an accurate picture in daylight. Note whatever adjustments you want to make, and wait until it's light again to change the display. Be careful when using a ladder outside; have a helper steady the ladder while you work.
- Every year, before setting up your illumination display, check light sets for cracked insulation, frayed wires or damaged sockets; all of these can cause short circuits.
- Don't overload string sets. Read the manufacturer's directions on each package to find out how many sets can be connected together.
- Avoid overloading circuits. Most home circuits can take 15 amps, or 1,800 watts. If you don't know your circuit capacity, play it safe and scale down your lighting display.
- Cover each outdoor plug and connector joint with plastic wrap to protect it from rain, sleet and snow; seal the wrapped joint carefully with electrical tape.
- If you use staples instead of tape to secure lights, be sure they're insulated staples.
- Make sure your decorations pose no danger to children or pets: Don't leave cords dangling, loose on the floor, or on the stairs.
- If you have questions about using decorative lights outdoors, you can call the GE Answer Center® information service 24 hours a day: 1-800-626-2000.

- Icicle lights are a pleasant change from the standard round or "flame" bulbs, but why stop there? There are strings of lights in all sorts of wild and whimsical shapes: carriage lamps, candles, even frogs and jalapeño peppers. Read the manufacturer's directions carefully before hanging light strings. If your novelty light set is not recommended for outdoor use, hang it indoors to frame a window.
- For a dramatic look to your outside lighting display, try floodlighting evergreens. Use blue, green, clear, or deluxe white mercury lamps—these colors enhance the colors of evergreens. Avoid using red, yellow, amber or pink lamps, which turn the trees a muddy brown color.
- Illuminate deciduous trees as well as evergreens. Flood a tree with a single spotlight to highlight its shape and pattern. Or place shiny ornaments on the tree, and light it from below with several smaller spotlights. If the tree is close enough to the house, use small lights for a festive look.
- Get more sparkle and glitter by using transparent bulbs. These, unlike color-coated bulbs, allow the filaments to show through.
- Use light bulb colors that are in the same color family. Blue and green are "cool colors." Red, orange, yellow and white are "warm colors."

GRAND ENTRANCE

This lovely lighting treatment makes the most of the unique architectural details of a house. You can adapt the same principles to your own home.

Easy: Achievable by anyone.

Materials: 2 small potted evergreen trees; evergreen garland; strings of clear, white medium-size lights; strings of blue miniature lights; green satin ribbon in widest width available.

Directions:
Using the photo as a guide, accent selected areas of the portico with the medium-size lights, spacing them widely. String medium-size lights on the potted trees, and place the trees on either side of the portico. String the miniature lights on larger shrubs in front of the house. Drape the evergreen garland over the entryway staircase banister, and tie the garland in place with green ribbon bows.

YULETIDE TABLE MAGIC

Greetings,
good master, mistress, children
Greetings, good health to one and all!
Once more we come to you with singing;
Open your door, we've come to call!
Let us now to your heart draw near
and with warmth and with food be welcomed!
—"Carol of the Mistletoe Singers"

At Christmas time
the dining table becomes the center of activity—after all,
no celebration is complete without a feast! Set a holiday
table with lovely linens and festive centerpieces.
Since holiday entertaining can range from buffet
breakfasts to elegant sit-down dinners, we've included
table-trimming ideas for a variety of occasions. Some are
as simple as a gathering of potted herbs, glass ball
ornaments, candles and napkins to make a homey
centerpiece. Others involve fancy cutwork or counted
cross stitch techniques to create lovely table linens.
Don't wait until Christmas Eve to set your holiday table.
These festive table toppers will delight your family and
friends at any meal of the season.

SET THE TABLE, SET THE MOOD

Greet your Christmas dinner guests with a
table as festive as the rest of your home.
From Victorian elegance to natural
simplicity, our table settings will help you
set the perfect tone for your feasting.

VICTORIAN SPARKLE TABLE SETTING

Easy: Achievable by anyone.

Materials: Green satin tablecloth; white lace-edged napkins; glass tabletop to fit dinner table; assorted antique or replica Christmas cards, postcards and paper ornaments; small gift boxes; gold doilies; gold metallic ribbon; little party favor gifts.

Directions:
1. Spread the tablecloth on the table. Place the Christmas cards, postcards, paper ornaments and doilies on top of the cloth in a pleasing arrangement *(see photo)*. Lay the glass top on the table to hold the decorations in place.
2. Tuck a little gift inside each box. Tie the boxes with the gold ribbon. Place a gold doily on top of each plate, and a gift box on each doily.
3. Fold the napkins in small squares and place them on the table so they hide as little of the decorations as possible *(see photo)*.

COLOR IT CHRISTMAS TABLE SETTING

Easy: Achievable by anyone.

Materials: Flower Ornaments (directions, at right); Christmas stocking; artificial red and white flowers; potted poinsettias; red candles in white candleholders; white lace table runner.

Directions:
Hang the ornaments from a chandelier or in front of a window. Spread the table runner across the table. Group the flowers in the stocking in a pleasing arrangement, and lay the stocking in the center of the table. Arrange the candles around the stocking. Place the poinsettias around the room.

FLOWER ORNAMENTS

Easy: Achievable by anyone.

Materials: Styrofoam® balls; white artificial flowers and green leaves; red strawflowers; white glue; ¼-inch-wide red satin ribbon for hangers; T-pins or hairpins.

Directions:
1. Glue the flowers and leaves all over the surface of the foam ball.
2. Cut the ribbon twice as long as the hanging length desired. With a T-pin or hairpin, fasten the center of the ribbon to the top of the ball and suspend the ornament.

HARVEST HOME TABLE SETTING

Easy: Achievable by anyone.

Materials: Hurricane lamp; wheat wreath; cranberries; twine; small wood cutting boards.

Directions:

Place the wreath around the hurricane lamp in the center of the table. Fill in the spaces with loose cranberries. Tie each napkin with a length of twine for a napkin ring. Use small cutting boards instead of individual dessert plates to serve a simple dessert of cheese and fruit.

TIPS FOR A "GREEN" CHRISTMAS

Dine by Candlelight

Set the most wonderful of moods and dine by candlelight. This adds intimacy, romance and instant beauty to any meal, and is especially nice during the holiday season. Best of all, it conserves a little energy during a time of year when you tend to use a lot of electricity.

SWEET CEDAR TABLE SETTING

Easy: Achievable by anyone.

Materials: Cuttings of fresh cedar; country-style place mats and matching napkins; stoneware plates; wooden napkin rings; chunky candles of various heights and colors.

Directions:
Set the place mats on the table and center a plate on each mat. Roll the napkins, place them in the napkin rings and set a ring with napkin on top of each plate. Spread the cedar cuttings around the place mats in a pleasing arrangement. Allow the cuttings to drape slightly across the place mats and over the table's edges. Place the candles among the cuttings.

CLEVER CRAFTING

Conversation Piece

A low centerpiece allows for a good flow of conversation across the table. The centerpiece should add to the overall look of the table, but it should never dominate. The stars of any meal should be taste-tempting food and cheerful company.

SIMPLE ELEGANCE HOLIDAY TABLE

Easy: Achievable by anyone.

Materials: Evergreen wreath; solid white tablecloth; white thread; sewing needle; wide red satin ribbon, or purchased large red satin bows with streamers; tall red candles; candleholders of various heights.

Directions:

1. If you are using red satin ribbon, make four large bows with long streamers. Place the tablecloth on the table. Gather the tablecloth at the center of one long side, and sew through the gathers to hold them in place *(see photo)*. Tack a bow over the stitches. If the table is long, gather the tablecloth twice along the side, and tack a bow over each set of gathers. Repeat on the other long side and two short ends of the table.

2. Place the wreath in the center of the table. Place the candles in the candleholders, and group them inside the wreath for a centerpiece.

TIPS FOR A "GREEN" CHRISTMAS

Natural Napkins

Changing over to reusable cloth napkins can dramatically cut down on your use of paper products. They're also more attractive and less expensive than paper napkins — a nice touch for family meals! Use them yourself, and give them as a "green" gift to neighbors and friends.

Here are some of our thoughts on how to turn ordinary cloth napkins into a beautiful Christmas gift; you'll probably come up with some creative ideas on your own.

● Buy a family-sized set of napkins and embroider the initials of each family member in the corner of "their" napkin.

● Give enough napkins for a week's worth of meals, so they all can be thrown in with the weekly laundry. Choose varying shades of a single color to match the recipient's decor, or offer a rainbow of different colors.

● Buy a set of napkins in a light color, and stencil a design on the corner of each napkin.

● Make napkins by hemming squares of fabric. Colorful floral prints, plaids or solids all make good choices. Or make a set of holiday napkins from fabrics for Easter, Valentine's Day, St. Patrick's Day, Halloween, Thanksgiving and, of course, Christmas!

● Roll the napkins and tie them with ribbons. Then group them in a pretty basket for giving.

● Accompany your gift of napkins with place mats, napkin rings or a book on napkin folding.

CENTERPIECES AND ACCENTS

Whether you revel in nature's bounty or
"go for the gilt," you can create a lovely
focal point for your holiday table. Or add
Christmas cheer to any corner of the house
with just the right accent.

POINSETTIA BASKET

(photos, page 21 and at left)

Easy: Achievable by anyone.

Materials: Basket with handle; potted red poinsettia; 2 to 4 gladioli; white lace-edged napkin; red satin ribbon; 2 small jars; floral foam; thin floral wire.

Directions:

1. Place the napkin in the basket, draping napkin corners over the basket's front and back edges. Place the poinsettia in the basket.

2. Wire an upright small jar on the inside of the basket at the bottom of each end of the basket handle. Fill the jars with floral foam.

3. Place one or two gladioli in each jar. Wire the gladiolus stems to the basket handle to cover it. Tie a red ribbon bow at each end of the handle.

CLEVER CRAFTING

Poinsettias

The following "holiday" schedule will make caring for a poinsettia very easy.

● Christmas season: As long as the plant is in bloom, keep it in a well-lighted spot (direct sunlight isn't necessary once it is past blooming), with evenly moist, not soggy, soil. Feed the poinsettia every two weeks, year-round, with a complete fertilizer, such as 10-15-10.

● St. Patrick's Day: Cut back the bracts. These are the large, brightly colored, modified leaves that are often mistakenly called flowers.

● Memorial Day: Repot the plant into a larger container and put the plant outdoors for the summer.

● Fourth of July: Cut the stems back by six inches.

● Labor Day: Move the plant indoors to a sunny window.

● Columbus Day: Begin giving the plant 14 hours of darkness daily. Poinsettias are photoperiodic — producing colorful bracts and blooms (the yellow berries in the center of the bracts) in response to shorter periods of daylight. Cover the plant with a box or place it in a closet; it must have absolute darkness.

Continue this treatment for 8 to 10 weeks. During the day, place the plant in a window where it will receive 4 to 6 hours of direct sun; water and feed as usual. As soon as the poinsettia comes into bloom, discontinue the treatment.

By following this schedule, you should have a colorful poinsettia again for Christmas.

CLEVER CRAFTING

Handy Arrangements

If you have these items on hand, you'll always be able to create "instant arrangements" for your table.

● Candles: A selection of tapers, chunk candles and votive candles in red, green and white with holders to match.

● Pretty bowls and baskets: They can give your table a theme — baskets say "country," a pewter bowl is distinctly Colonial, ornate china or crystal bowls are elegant, stoneware adds a homey touch.

● Pine cones: Large and small, paint them, wire them, glue them, roll them in glitter, tie them with bows or simply toss them in a pretty container.

● Fruit: Fill a bowl or basket with bright green apples, red apples or citrus for a pretty and fragrant centerpiece.

● Ball ornaments: Use them as you would fresh fruit. They make a simple, sparkling centerpiece.

● Mirror: Lay it flat on the table and place your arrangement on top, the mirror will reflect candlelight or give a simple arrangement more presence.

HERB GARDEN CENTERPIECE

Easy: Achievable by anyone.

Materials: Large wooden salad bowl; variety of potted herbs, such as parsley, sage, dwarf sage, rosemary, oregano and scented geranium; additional fresh parsley; red striped or checked dishtowel; 3 red striped or checked napkins; red glass ball ornaments in assorted sizes; three 10-inch-tall dripless red candles; 3 candle pins *(metal disc with spike in middle; optional)*; 6 wooden napkin rings; empty medicine bottles; heavy-duty aluminum foil.

Directions:

1. Centerpiece: Line the salad bowl with a piece of aluminum foil. Cover the foil with the dishtowel, draping the corners of the towel over the edge of the bowl.

2. Arrange the potted herbs in the bowl. Fill the medicine bottles with water, and place a clump of fresh parsley in each bottle. Fill in the spaces around the potted herbs with the bottled parsley; the parsley will last for 2 to 3 days. Place the bowl in the center of the table. Group the ball ornaments into clusters around the bowl to imitate fruit.

3. Candleholders: Stack two napkin rings. Place a candle in the center of a napkin, and push them both into the stacked rings so the napkin gathers into petals. Separate the stacked rings slightly. Repeat with the remaining candles, napkins and napkin rings. If a candle needs to be steadied, press its bottom onto a candle pin. Arrange the candles around the centerpiece.

GOLDEN ANGEL

Average: For those with some experience in crafting.

Materials: ½ yard of 36-inch-wide solid white or pastel cotton fabric; matching thread; 14 x 8 inches of scrim or stiff cotton tulle; 1 yard of narrow lace trim; ½ yard of ¼-inch-wide ribbon; 2-inch-long Styrofoam® egg; scraps of 4-ply yarn; 1 pair of long false eyelashes; 12-inch square of heavy cardboard; 12-inch-wide manila folder or other lightweight cardboard; wire coat hanger; gold spray paint; gold glitter; liquid starch; sewing needle; ¾-inch-wide plastic strapping tape; stapler; all-purpose glue; wax paper; paper for pattern.

Directions:

1. Cover the heavy cardboard square with wax paper, and use it as a working surface. From the manila folder or other lightweight cardboard, make a 12-inch-long cone with a 4-inch-diameter base for the angel body. Staple and tape the overlapping edges together. Impale and glue the Styrofoam egg on the point of the cone for the angel head.

2. Cut a 14-inch length from the straight section of the wire hanger. Bend and shape the wire to form the angel shoulders, bent arms, and hands *(see photo)*. Holding the shoulder piece at the base of the head, secure the piece very firmly in place by winding strapping tape several times over and around the wire and body, and around the base of the head.

3. Enlarge the pattern in FIG. II, 1 *(page 34)* onto paper, following the directions on page 271. Place the dotted line of the Dress pattern along a folded edge of paper, cut out and open for a full pattern. Cut out the Wings and Collar pattern pieces. Fold the cotton fabric into an 18-inch square. Place the top edge of the Dress pattern on the fabric fold, and cut out the Dress through the double thickness fabric. Cut out the Collar from a single thickness of the same fabric. Cut a 2-inch-long opening down the center back of the Dress. Cut a 1¼-inch-long opening down the center back of the Collar. Turn in the hems. Sew lengths of lace trim around the sleeve edges and the bottom edge of the Collar. Right sides in, sew the Dress side/sleeve seams; turn the Dress right side out.

4. Pour some undiluted liquid starch into a bowl. Saturate the Dress in the starch, and squeeze out the excess starch. Place the Dress carefully on the angel, threading the wire arms through the sleeves. Drape the Dress into graceful folds, and turn under about 1 inch at the Dress bottom. Place the Collar around the neck, with the opening at the back, and secure the Collar at the back of the neck with small stitches. Tie the ribbon firmly around the angel's waist for a sash.

5. Cut approximately fifty 6-inch-long strands of yarn. Dip the strands into the starch, and arrange them on the angel's head to resemble hair. Trim the strand ends neatly around the angel's face and forehead to make rounded bangs.

6. Soak a 6-inch length of lace trim in the starch, and arrange the lace upright on top of the angel head as a coronet.

7. Cut each false eyelash into two ¼-inch sections. Glue the sections to the face as eyes *(see photo)*.

8. Let the angel dry completely; it may take several days. When the angel is completely dry, cut the Wings from the scrim or tulle. Clip, overlap, and staple each Wing in place to make a graceful curving shape *(see Wings pattern piece in* FIG. II, 1*)*. Lift the hair away from the angel's back gently but firmly, and insert the Wings underneath the hair so the Wings' flat center section is just below the top of the angel's shoulder blades. Glue the Wings in place securely.

9. Make a 4-inch-long cone with a 1-inch-diameter base from the manila folder for the trumpet. Staple and tape the overlapping edges together. Wrap tape around the ends of the angel's wire arms to form the hands. Glue the trumpet to the angel's hands, and to the angel's face at the mouth.

10. Spray several coats of gold paint over the completed angel to cover every crack and crevice, letting the paint dry between coats. After the last coat, sprinkle the trumpet with gold glitter before the paint dries.

FIG. II, 1 GOLDEN ANGEL   1 SQ. = 1"

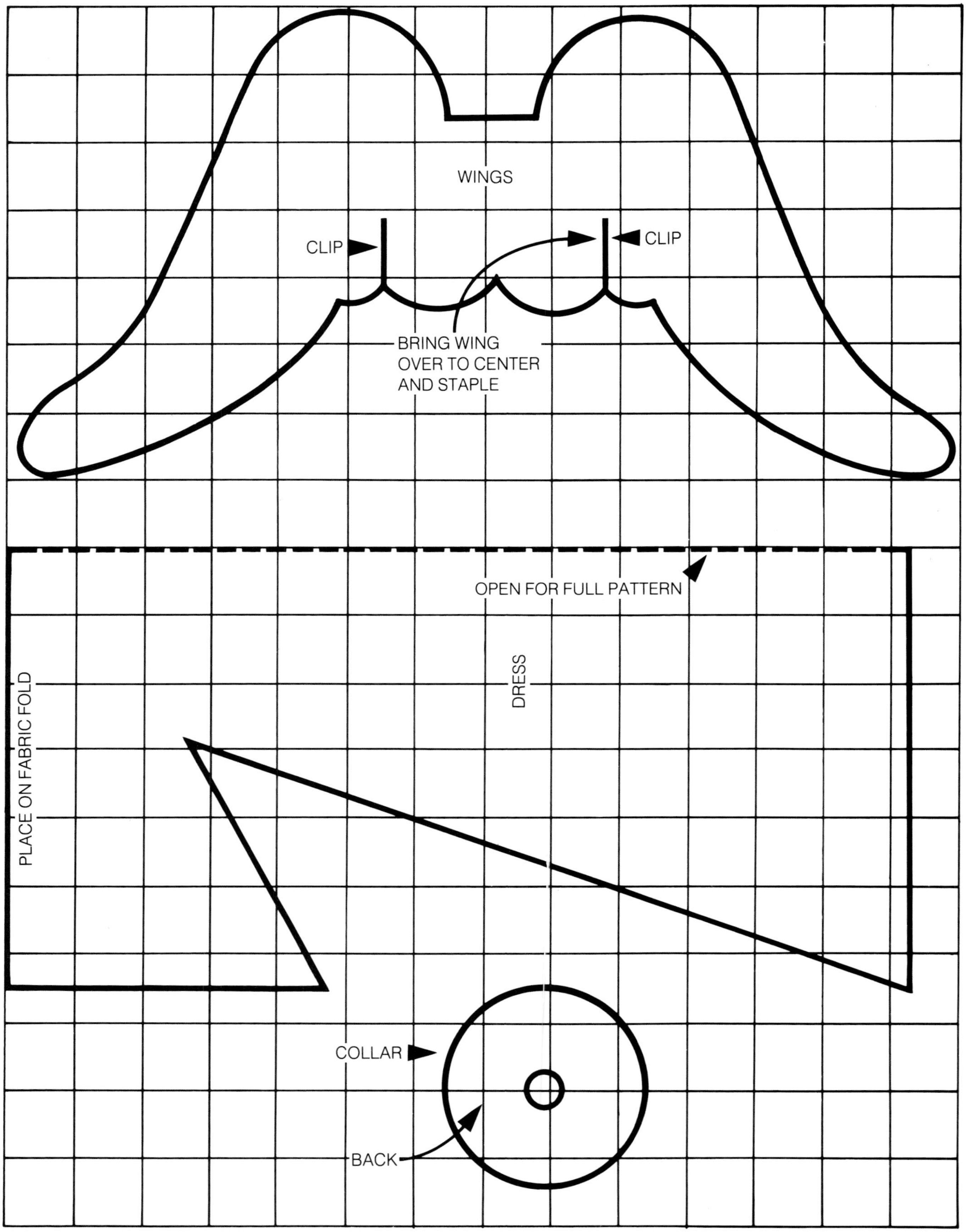

WINGS

CLIP ▶

◀ CLIP

BRING WING
OVER TO CENTER
AND STAPLE

OPEN FOR FULL PATTERN

PLACE ON FABRIC FOLD

DRESS

COLLAR ▶

BACK

GOLDEN VINES WREATH

Without the candleholders, this also makes a lovely door decoration.

Easy: Achievable by anyone.

Materials: Plain grapevine wreath; artificial ivy; pine cones; clip-on candleholders with red candles; gold paint or spray paint; floral wire.

Directions:

1. Spray paint the ivy gold. Or pour gold paint into a dish, and dip the ivy leaves into the paint. Let the paint dry.

2. Wire the ivy around the wreath. Wrap a length of floral wire around the base of each pine cone. Then wire the pine cones, evenly spaced, around the wreath.

3. Space the candleholders evenly around the wreath, and clip them to the wreath securely. Make sure the candleholders sit straight on the wreath, so they can catch the wax drippings from the burning candles.

4. Place the wreath in the center of the table, and light the candles. Do not leave the centerpiece unattended while the candles are burning.

CLEVER CRAFTING

Pine Cone Pointer

Before using pine cones for wreaths or other Christmas decorations, place them in a warm oven for about an hour. The heat makes them open up.

HOLIDAY TABLE LINENS

Whether you're having a family breakfast
on Christmas morning or a lavish Christmas
Eve supper, dress your table beautifully
with special holiday table linens.

FANCY CUTWORK TABLECLOTH
(about 54 inches square)

Challenging: Requires more experience in sewing or embroidering.

General Materials: 1½ yards of 54-inch-wide linen; washable or disappearing fabric marker; black fine-point permanent felt tip pen; sharp-point embroidery scissors; white paper; tracing paper for pattern.

General Directions:

1. The tablecloth can be embroidered by machine *(see photo)*, or by hand. Directions are given for both hand and machine methods.

2. Straighten the raw edges of the linen to form a perfect 54-inch square. Enlarge the corner motif half pattern in FIG. II, 2A *(page 38)* onto folded tracing paper, following the directions on page 169. Trace the motif onto the other half of the paper, and open the paper for the full motif. Enlarge the center motif quarter pattern in FIG. II, 2B *(page 39)* onto tracing paper folded into quarters; place the paper folds on the pattern center lines. Trace the motif onto the remaining quarters, and open the paper for the full motif. Go over the lines of the full motifs with the black felt tip pen.

3. Place white paper under the center motif. Center the linen square over the center motif; the motif should show through the linen clearly. Trace the motif onto the linen with the washable or disappearing fabric marker. Repeat with the corner motif on the linen corners.

4. If you use a washable fabric marker, when you have finished embroidering the tablecloth, remove remaining motif tracings following the washable fabric marker manufacturer's instructions. Dry the tablecloth, and press it.

MACHINE-SEWN TABLECLOTH
Materials: General Materials; 2 yards of tear-away stabilizer; 15 spools of red machine embroidery thread; 1 pack of size 90 Schmetz universal needles; pins.

Directions:

1. Prepare the linen following General Directions, Steps 2 and 3.

2. Place a large square of tear-away stabilizer under the center motif, and pin it in place. Repeat at each corner, extending the stabilizer 1 inch beyond the edges of the linen for ease of stitching.

3. Use a new needle in the sewing machine. Wind several bobbins with the red thread. Select a 2-mm-wide, 2-mm-long zigzag stitch. Decrease the presser foot pressure two to three notches. Decrease the upper thread tension two to three notches.

4. Zigzag stitch over all the design lines of the center motif except the richelieu lines, which are the connecting threads between the open spaces. Plan a stitching route, rather than jumping from spot to spot. When jumping is unavoidable, lift the presser foot, slide the linen to the new location without cutting the threads, and continue stitching. Clip the needle and bobbin threads last.

5. Cut out the linen cutwork areas with the embroidery scissors, leaving the richelieu lines in place; do not cut the tear-away stabilizer.

6. Decrease the stitch length and width to 1 mm. Start the richelieu stitching 1 mm to 2 mm in from the linen cutwork edges to secure the stitching. Stitch on the richelieu lines across the cutwork areas, stitching through the tear-away stabilizer. Press the reverse button on the machine, and stitch back over the first layer of richelieu stitching.

7. Work the vein lines on the leaves in buttonhole stitch *(see* FIGS. II, 2A *and* 2B, *and photo)*. Work the flower centers in tapered satin stitch *(see* FIGS. II, 2A *and* 2B, *and photo)*.

Then decrease the stitch length to ⁴/₁₀ mm, increase the stitch width to 3 mm, and check the bobbin thread. Satin stitch around all the cutwork areas; the left swing of the needle will fall off the linen into the tear-away stabilizer, and the right swing of the needle will fall into the linen, covering the previous stitching completely. For a more natural look, stitch the background areas first, then the foreground areas. Use tapered satin stitch to stitch into angles and corners. When the embroidering is completed, pull the tear-away stabilizer carefully away from the linen, then from the cutwork, being careful not to tear the delicate richelieu lines. Trim stray threads.

8. Dust the bobbin and feed teeth area. Change the needle. Repeat Steps 3 through 7 on each corner.

9. Insert a buttonhole presser foot. Select a 3-mm-wide, ⁴/₁₀-mm-long zigzag stitch. With each edge of the linen square following the center of the foot, stitch to form a rolled satin stitch hem. Stitch twice. Remove remaining motif tracings following General Directions, Step 4.

EMBROIDERED TABLECLOTH
Materials: General Materials; red pearl cotton or embroidery floss; embroidery hoop; embroidery needle.

Directions:

1. Prepare the linen following General Directions, Steps 2 and 3, using a washable fabric marker.

2. Place the linen square in the embroidery hoop. Using the embroidery needle and pearl cotton or 3 strands of embroidery floss, outline the design lines of the center and corner motifs with a running stitch *(see Stitch Guide, page 168)*. As you come to one of the richelieu lines, which are the connecting threads between the open spaces,

Continued on page 39

CENTER

FIG. II, 2B   CENTER MOTIF—QUARTER PATTERN   1 SQ. = 1″

CENTER

carry the floss across the space to the opposite side, take a stitch, carry the floss back, take another stitch in the same place on the first side, and repeat to stretch three threads across the area.

3. When the motifs have been outlined, complete the richelieu lines by working buttonhole stitches over the three threads of each line, being careful not to catch the linen underneath the threads that will be cut away *(see Stitch Guide, page 168).* When the richelieu lines are completed, work buttonhole stitches over the design outlining stitches so

the ridge formed by each buttonhole stitch lies along the edge to be cut.

4. Work the vein lines on the leaves in blanket stitch. Work the flower centers in satin stitch *(see Stitch Guide, and* FIGS. II, 2A *and* 2B*).*

5. Make an X in all the linen areas to be cut away. Turn over the linen square, and cut out the areas from the wrong side with the embroidery scissors. Be careful not to cut into the buttonhole stitches.

6. Hem the edges of the linen square with buttonhole stitches. Remove remaining motif tracings following General Directions, Step 4 *(page 37).*

WINTER VILLAGE STENCILED TABLECLOTH & NAPKINS

Easy: Achievable by anyone.

Materials: Purchased solid white or ivory tablecloth and napkins untreated for soil resistance; Stencil-Ease® "Miniature Township" and "Sleigh Ride" stencils, or Mylar® (available at craft supply stores) or acetate sheets (available at art supply stores), black fine-point permanent felt tip pen, craft or utility knife, cardboard, piece of glass with taped edges, or piece of acrylic (available at home centers), masking tape, transparent tape, and artist's flat paintbrush; Fab-Tex® fabric stenciling paints: Barn Red, Country Blue, Slate Blue, Telemark Green, Colonial Gold and Historic Brown, or the colors of your choice; six No. 10 or 12 stencil brushes; paper toweling; paper; newspaper *(optional)*; cotton rags *(optional)*; rubbing alcohol *(optional)*.

Directions:

1. If you are making your own stencils, use the photo as a design guide to draw a simple sleigh, horse, tree and three or four different houses on paper. Cut a piece of Mylar or acetate an inch larger than each shape. Tape the acetate over the shape with masking tape. Trace the shape onto the acetate with the black felt tip pen. Using the cardboard, piece of glass with taped edges, or piece of acrylic as a cutting board, cut out the traced stencil shapes with the craft or utility knife. Pull the knife toward you, and cut in a continuous motion. If a stencil shape needs to be turned, turn the acetate rather than the knife. Once the knife tip pierces the acetate, do not lift the tip again until you have finished cutting the line or curve. If you make a mistake or the acetate tears, repair the spot with a piece of transparent tape.

2. Wash the tablecloth and napkins to remove sizing, and iron them.

3. Place the tablecloth on a hard surface. Place several layers of paper toweling underneath the tablecloth where you will start stenciling. Using your own or the purchased stencils, and the photo as a color and placement guide, stencil houses, trees, and a horse and sleigh around the tablecloth to resemble an old-fashioned village scene. If you are using the "Miniature Township" stencil, use the evergreen trees, and stencil the mountains lightly in Country Blue to suggest a winter scene. If you are using your own stencils, paint the mountains freehand with an artist's flat paintbrush.

4. Tape the top of the first stencil in place with masking tape. If the shape uses more than one color, mask off all the cut outs except for the first color by taping paper under them. Holding a stencil brush like a pencil, dip it into the first color stencil paint. Using an up-and-down pouncing motion, pounce the brush on folded paper toweling or newspaper until the brush is almost dry. Pounce the brush on the open stencil cut outs, starting at the cut edges. Stencil the cut outs from the outside in so the center of the shape is lighter colored than the edges. Let the paint dry. Mask off those cut outs. Repeat with the remaining colors for the shape. Use a different stencil brush for each color used. Repeat with the other stencils, changing the paper toweling padding under the tablecloth each time you start a different shape. Wrap the stencil brushes in plastic wrap, or self-sealing plastic bags, to prevent the paint from drying on the brushes before you are finished stenciling. Clean the stencils when the paint starts to build up on them, to prevent paint build-up from distorting the stencil shapes.

5. Stencil a house, with evergreen trees on either side of it, in a corner of each napkin; use a different house for each napkin.

6. Clean the stencils with paper toweling or cotton rags soaked in soapy water or rubbing alcohol. Pat the stencils dry. Store the stencils flat or between layers of cardboard. Clean the stencil brushes with soap and water until the rinse water runs clear. Let the brushes dry completely before using them again.

7. Allow the stenciling to cure overnight. Set the stenciling with heat following the stencil paint manufacturer's instructions.

CROSS STITCH COUNTRY MAT

Average: For those with some experience in counted cross stitch.

Materials: 12-inch square of green 14-count Aida cloth; embroidery floss: 2 skeins of White, and 1 skein each of Medium Pink, Red, Coral, Dark Orange, Royal Blue, Gold and Dark Brown; tapestry needle; sewing needle; embroidery hoop.

Directions:

1. Find and pin mark the center lines of the cloth. Place the cloth in the hoop. Using two strands of floss in the tapestry needle, cross stitch the design in FIG. II, 3 centered on the cloth *(see Stitch Guide, page 168).* Each symbol in FIG. II, 3 represents one cross stitch in the color indicated. The row outside the border is 1 inch in from the edge of the cloth. Begin and end each floss length by running it through stitches on the back.

2. When the stitching is completed,

block the mat, right side down, using a pressing cloth and steam iron.

3. Trim the edges of the mat 1 inch

beyond the row outside the border. Turn under the edges of the mat 1 inch all around, press, and hem them.

FIG. II, 3 CROSS STITCH COUNTRY MAT

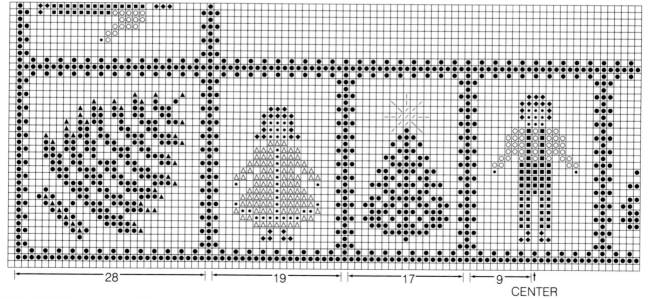

28   19   17   9

CENTER

● = WHITE   ⊡ = MEDIUM PINK   ▲ = RED
■ = ROYAL BLUE   △ = CORAL   ⊟ = GOLD
◆ = DARK BROWN   ◎ = DARK ORANGE

42

"HAPPY HOLIDAYS" CROSS STITCH TABLE RUNNER

(13 x 26⅜ inches)

Average: For those with some experience in counted cross stitch.

Materials: 18 x 32 inches of white 14-count Aida cloth; matching sewing thread; embroidery floss: 6 skeins of Red, 4 skeins of Light Green, 2 skeins each of Medium Green and Dark Green, and 1 skein each of Pink, Dark Red, Blue, Yellow and Brown; tapestry needle; sewing needle; embroidery hoop.

Directions:

1. The outer dimensions of the embroidered area are 12½ x 25¾ inches. Find the center lines of the Aida cloth, and pin mark them. Place the Aida cloth in the embroidery hoop. Using three strands of floss in the tapestry needle, cross stitch a motif of your choice in FIG. II, 4 *(page 44)* centered on the Aida cloth *(see Stitch Guide, page 168)*. Each symbol in FIG. II, 4 represents one cross stitch in the color indicated. Then cross stitch the other motifs, arranging and repeating the motifs on the grid as you like and alternating them with empty grid squares *(see photo)*.

Work the straight dark grid lines in Red backstitch. Work the straight lines around the lights on the corner Christmas trees in Yellow backstitch *(see Stitch Guide)*. Begin and end each length of floss by running it through stitches on the back of the work.

2. When the cross stitching is completed, press the runner, right side down, with a damp cloth to block it. Hem the runner to the finished size, and press it again.

FIG. II, 4 "HAPPY HOLIDAYS" CROSS STITCH TABLE RUNNER

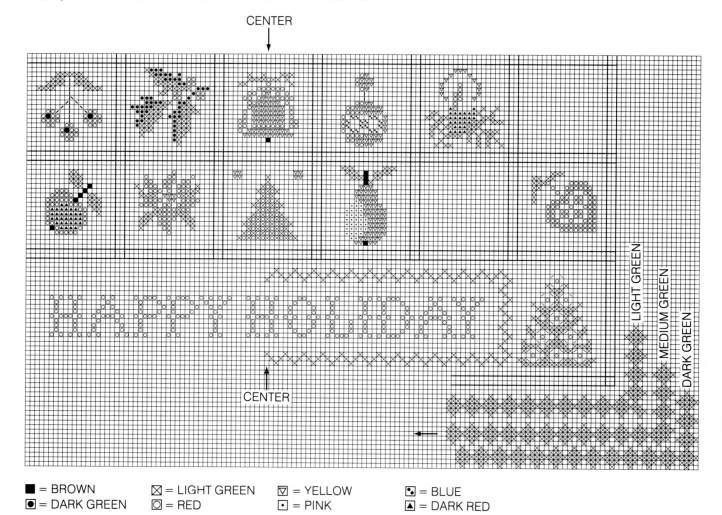

■ = BROWN ⊠ = LIGHT GREEN ▽ = YELLOW ⊡ = BLUE

⊙ = DARK GREEN ⊡ = RED ⊡ = PINK ▲ = DARK RED

CHRISTMAS MORNING PLACE SETTINGS

Average: For those with some experience in sewing.

Materials for Each Place Mat:
24 x 17 inches of fabric for mat top; 21½ x 14½ inches of coordinating fabric for mat back; 60 inches of ½-inch-wide red braid; 60 inches of ½-inch-wide green braid; matching threads; sewing needle. ***For Each Napkin:*** 22½ x 21½ inches of place mat back fabric. ***For Each Napkin Ring:*** 18 inches of 1½-inch-wide red grosgrain ribbon; 4-inch dark green frog closure.

Directions:
1. Place Mat: Turn under the edges of the place mat top ¼ inch all around, then 1 inch, and press. Place the place mat back on the place mat top, wrong sides together, and tuck the back's raw edges underneath the top's folded edge. Topstitch through all the layers using the inside folded edge as a stitch guide. Turn over the place mat. Place the red braid on the place mat top, using the stitchline as a guide. Slipstitch the braid in place. Repeat with the green braid, lapping it slightly over the red braid's inside edge *(see photo)*.
2. Napkin: Turn under the edges of the fabric ¼ inch all around, then 1 inch, and press. Stitch, mitering the corners.
3. Napkin Ring: Knot the ribbon, leaving a loop for the napkin to fit through. Cut the ribbon ends into fish tails. Stitch the frog closure over the ribbon knot.

ALL THROUGH THE HOUSE

Mistletoe
hung from the gas brackets
in all the front parlors;
there was sherry and walnuts
and bottled beer and crackers
by the dessertspoons;
and cats in their fur-abouts watched the fires;
and the high-heaped fire spat,
all ready for the chestnuts
and the mulling pokers.
—Dylan Thomas

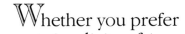

Whether you prefer
Victorian finery or the sweet simplicity of Americana,
you'll find a wealth of holiday trims and decorations in
this chapter. You can carry a theme throughout the
house, or select your favorite elements to mix with your
family treasures.
Fill your home with Victorian splendor: there are dainty
crepe flowers for piling in pretty bowls or trimming your
tree to rich velvet stockings and floppy velveteen rabbits.
If your heart is "in country," try our cheery peppermint-
striped ornaments, down-home stockings or lovely balsa
wood nativity scene.
There's also a wonderful selection of Santa ornaments
and wooden figures for your tree.
Let the spirit of Christmas spill into every room and
corner of your home!

GRAND VICTORIANA

Enchant your family and friends with the opulence of a Victorian-style Christmas. Dazzle the eye with delicate crepe paper flowers brightened by leaves of green satin and holiday plaid taffeta ribbons. Bedeck your tree with these pretties, adorn a wreath or pile the flowers in a beautiful porcelain bowl. Create sumptuous stockings from chintz and velvet, or stitch up a velveteen rabbit to make this Christmas just grand!

CREPE PAPER FLOWERS WITH BOWS

Average: For those with some experience in crafting.

Materials: 1 package of off-white extra-strength crepe paper (enough to make 8 to 9 flowers); red and medium green regular crepe paper; 1 yard of plaid taffeta; matching thread; 1½-inch-wide apple green satin ribbon; small red sequins; No. 26 green covered wire; No. 19 stem wire; green floral tape; clear acrylic spray varnish; small watercolor paintbrush; red wide felt tip marker; black fine-point permanent felt tip pen; rubbing alcohol; extra-large cotton cosmetic puffs; waxed dental floss; toothpicks; needlenose pliers; wire cutters; scissors; white glue; newspapers.

Directions:

1. Flower Center: Make a small hook at one end of a 6-inch length of stem wire. Pull the wire through a cotton puff, catching the hook inside the puff. Cut a 4-inch square of red crepe paper, and cover the cotton puff with it. Wind a 6-inch length of dental floss tightly around the base of the covered puff to secure the crepe paper. Make dots on the crepe paper with the black fine-point pen.

2. Cutting across the grain, cut a 2 x 8-inch strip of medium green crepe paper. Fringe the strip's long edges with the scissors. Fasten one short end of the strip to the base of the flower center with a dot of glue. Wind the strip around the base, and glue the loose end to the base.

3. Petals: Cut the package of extra-strength crepe paper crosswise into five equal parts. Cut each part in half lengthwise *(see* FIG. III, 1A*).* Round off the corners at one short end of each paper bundle to make petals *(see* FIG. III, 1B*).* Color each rounded petal edge with the red marker. Touch the colored area with the watercolor brush dipped in the alcohol, so the color will run and soften. Let the petals dry. Ripple the rounded petal edges by stretching them gently between your fingers.

4. Double Petal Flower: Space four petals evenly around the flower center, and wind a 12-inch length of dental floss around the base of the flower to secure them. Space four more petals evenly around the flower center. Pulling tightly, wind all the floss around the base; it isn't necessary to tie the floss. Cup the base of each outside petal slightly by stretching it gently between your thumbs and forefingers. Using a toothpick, glue six to eight sequins to the flower center.

5. Single Petal Flower: Assemble the flower following Step 4, using only four petals.

6. Green Bow: Using an 18-inch length of satin ribbon, make 2¼-inch-long double ribbon loops, and crimp the loops in the center. Using the pliers, twist a 5-inch length of covered wire tightly around the crimped center. Attach the bow to the base of the flower with the covered wire, and wrap the excess covered wire around the flower stem.

7. Plaid Bow: Place the taffeta on a sheet of newspaper. Size the taffeta by spraying it with two light coats of acrylic, letting the acrylic dry briefly between coats. Let the sized taffeta dry completely. Cut 1¾-inch-wide taffeta bias strips, and sew their ends together. Cut a 48-inch length from the pieced strip. Leaving a 5-inch-long tail, make a 3-inch-long plaid loop and crimp the base between your fingers. Wrap a 12-inch length of covered wire once around the base. Make a second loop, and wrap the base with the wire. Repeat until there are five loops. Attach the plaid bow to the base of the flower, opposite the green bow, and wrap the excess covered wire around the flower stem. Wrap the flower stem with floral tape. Use the stem to attach the flower to a tree or wreath.

FIG. III, 1A   CREPE PAPER FLOWERS WITH BOWS

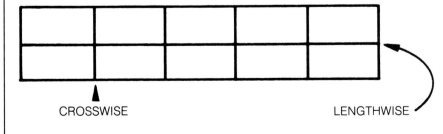

CROSSWISE   LENGTHWISE

FIG. III, 1B

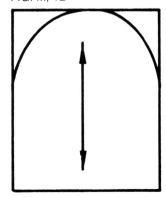

VICTORIANA WREATH

Average: For those with some experience in crafting.

Materials: 3 Crepe Paper Flowers with Bows *(directions, page 49)*; grapevine or straw wreath; dried baby's breath; 1¾-inch-wide plaid taffeta ribbon; floral wire; wire cutters.

Directions:

1. Divide the baby's breath into small bunches. Tie each bunch with floral wire, leaving the wire ends free.

2. Make plaid bows following Crepe Paper Flowers with Bows, Step 7 *(page 49)*, using the plaid taffeta ribbon and floral wire in place of the fabric and covered wire, and omitting the sizing. Wire several of the bows together into a cluster, leaving the wire ends free. Repeat with the remaining bows.

3. Using the wire ends, attach the plaid bow clusters around the outside edge of the grapevine or straw wreath. Attach the baby's breath to the front of the wreath to cover it completely *(see photo)*.

4. Using the photo as a placement guide, attach the Crepe Paper Flowers with Bows to one side of the wreath.

A PRETTY BOWL OF POSIES

Average: For those with some experience in crafting.

Materials: Porcelain bowl; Crepe Paper Flowers with Bows *(Directions, page 49)*; baby's breath; narrow red satin ribbon.

Directions:
Divide the baby's breath into small bunches, and tie each bunch with a long length of ribbon to make a nosegay. Arrange the Crepe Paper Flowers with Bows in the bowl, mounding them in the center. Fill in with the nosegays, letting their ribbon ends hang over the edge of the bowl.

TIPS FOR A "GREEN" CHRISTMAS

Recyclable Arts and Crafts

When the kids are home for Christmas vacation, you can be sure of having at least one foul-weather day. Be prepared! Collect various throwaway items that can be turned into arts and crafts. This way, you'll not only be ready for rainy-day activities, you'll be recycling as well.

Here are some throwaways that can be recycled into works of art.
- Plastic foam meat trays
- Plastic foam egg cartons
- Spools
- Old magazines
- Yarn scraps
- Buttons
- Beads and sequins

FIG. III, 2   DAINTY MINI-STOCKING

FULL SIZE PATTERN

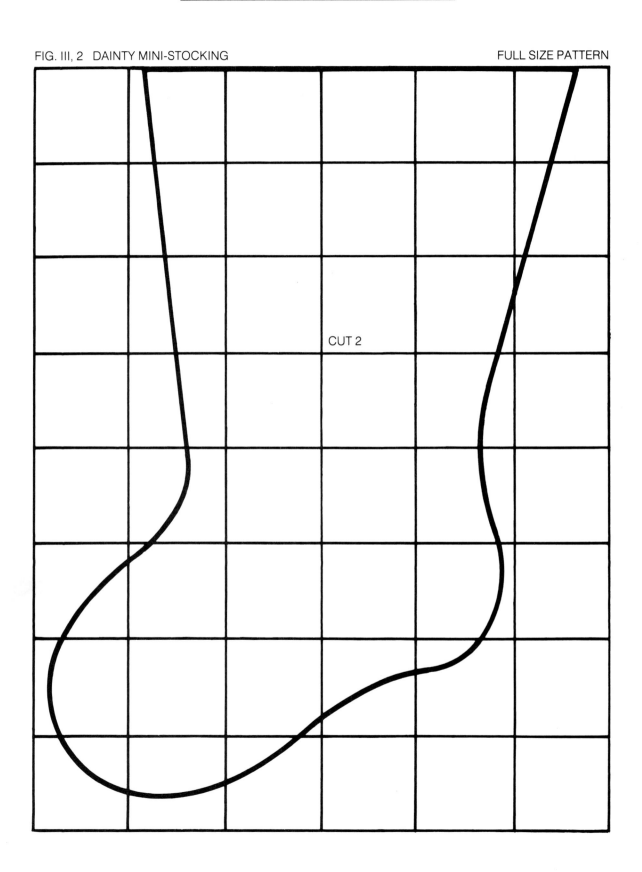

CUT 2

DAINTY MINI-STOCKING

Average: For those with some experience in sewing.

Materials: ⅓ yard of floral print fabric; matching thread; coordinating color ribbon; old or purchased crocheted round doily; old or purchased lace; fusible interfacing; tracing paper for pattern.

Directions
(¼-inch seams allowed):

1. Trace the full-size stocking pattern in Fig. III, 2 onto paper.

2. Cut out two stockings each from the floral print fabric and interfacing. Fuse each interfacing stocking to the wrong side of a fabric stocking. Stitch the fabric stockings right sides together, leaving the top edge open. Clip the curves, and turn the stocking right side out.

3. Fold the doily in half twice, and pin mark the center point. Open the doily halfway. Pin mark on the fold 2 inches on either side of the center. Remove the center pin. Cut along the fold between the pins.

4. With right sides together and edges matching, pin the cut edge of the doily to the top edge of the stocking. Using a ½-inch seam allowance, stitch around the top edge of the stocking. Turn the seam allowance to the inside, and stitch ¼ inch from the raw edges through all thicknesses except the doily.

5. Tack the ribbon and lace bows around the front top edge of the stocking *(see photo)*. Fold a length of ribbon in half, and tack the raw ends to the stocking's inside back seam for a hanger loop.

VELVETEEN RABBITS

*(small rabbit: 6 inches tall, seated;
large rabbit: 12 inches tall, seated)*

Average: For those with some
experience in sewing.

Materials: 45-inch-wide velveteen:
⅜ yard for small rabbit, and ¾ yard
for large rabbit; matching sewing
thread; heavy duty button thread; gold
cording; small jingle bells; artificial
pine sprigs; synthetic stuffing; sewing
needle; paper for patterns.

Directions
(¼-inch seams allowed):

1. Patterns: Enlarge the small rabbit
pattern in FIG. III, 3 onto paper
following the directions on page 169,
and using the ratio given. Enlarge the
large rabbit pattern onto a separate
sheet of paper using the larger ratio.

2. Cutting: For each rabbit, cut one
pair of Body pieces and two pairs
each of Arm, Leg and Ear pieces from
the velveteen.

3. Stitching: Sew each pair of Body,
Arm, Leg and Ear pieces right sides
together, leaving an opening for
turning between the circles. Clip the
curves where indicated. Turn the
Body, Arms and Legs right side out,
and stuff them. Turn in their open
edges, and slipstitch the openings
closed *(see Stitch Guide, page 168)*.

4. Ears: Turn the Ears right side out.
Gather their open edges slightly, and
slipstitch them to the Body at the ear
positions *(see dotted line on Body
pattern in FIG. III, 3)*.

5. Assembling: Using the heavy duty
button thread, sew the Arms and Legs
to the Body, matching X's; take several
stitches from each Arm or Leg to the
Body so the limbs can move.

6. Face: Using the heavy duty thread,
make a French knot for each eye as
indicated on the pattern *(see Stitch
Guide)*. Thread the needle with three
lengths of heavy duty thread. Push the
needle into the whiskers mark on one
side of the head, and out at the
whiskers mark on the other side of
the head *(see Body pattern)*. Knot the
threads against each side of the head,
and cut the thread ends to 3 inches.

7. Trims: For each rabbit, cut a
length of gold cording and sew a
jingle bell to each end. Tie the
cording around the rabbit's neck, and
tuck a pine sprig under the cording.

FIG. III, 3 VELVETEEN RABBITS

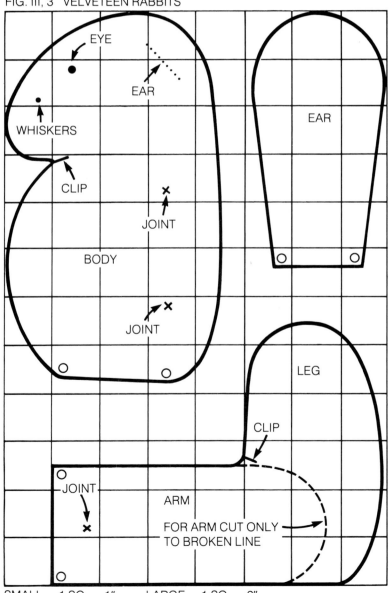

EYE

EAR

WHISKERS

EAR

CLIP

JOINT ×

BODY

JOINT ×

LEG

CLIP

JOINT ×

ARM

FOR ARM CUT ONLY
TO BROKEN LINE

SMALL — 1 SQ. = 1"   LARGE — 1 SQ. = 2"

pieces. Clip the curves, and turn the velvet stockings right side out. If you wish, hand-sew narrow braid along the velvet stockings' outside seams.

4. Cut the cuff braid 1 inch longer than the stocking's top edge. Stitch the short ends together ½ inch from their raw edges. If you wish, stitch narrow braids to the cuff's edges. Pin the right side of the cuff to the wrong side of the velvet stocking, back seams matching. Stitch the cuff to the stocking. Turn the cuff to the outside.

5. Fold a 7-inch length of braid in half; stitch the ends to the stocking's inside back seam for a hanger.

6. Insert a lining into each stocking, seams matching. Turn under the raw top edge; slipstitch the lining to the stocking *(see Stitch Guide, page 168).*

FIG. III, 4   VICTORIAN
VELVET STOCKINGS

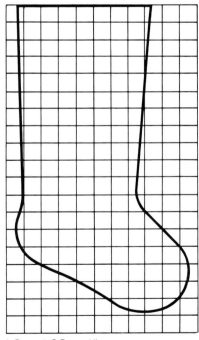

LG. — 1 SQ. = 1"
MED. — 1 SQ. = ¾"
SM. — 1 SQ. = ½"

VELVET STOCKINGS
(9, 13½ and 18 inches long)

Average: For those with some experience in sewing.

Materials: 44-inch-wide fabric: ¾ yard each of velvet and lining; selection of woven and metallic braids in various widths, including enough 2-inch-wide or wider woven braid to fit around top edge of each stocking for a cuff; matching threads; sewing needle; paper for patterns.

Directions
(¼-inch seams allowed):

1. Enlarge the pattern in FIG. III, 4 onto paper following the directions on page 169, making a pattern for each size stocking using the ratios given. For each stocking, cut a pair of pieces from the velvet and the lining.

2. Using the photo as a guide, arrange the woven and metallic braids on the right side of each velvet stocking. Topstitch the braids in place.

3. Stitch each pair of velvet stockings, right sides together, leaving the top edges open. Repeat with the lining

A CONTEMPORARY COUNTRY CHRISTMAS

Blend old and new by creating a country-warm holiday in a
modern setting. Just adding a few simple touches can turn a
contemporary room into a cozy, old-fashioned retreat. Quilts,
old or new, quilted pillows, afghans or blankets all add
Christmas cheer, particularly when they are brightly colored.
Use lots of red and white and pick up the colors of the room in
your tree ornaments.

PEPPERMINT-STRIPED ORNAMENTS

Easy: Achievable by anyone.

Materials: Balsa wood; craft knife; fine sandpaper; variety of Christmas cookie cutters; red and white acrylic paints; masking tape; narrow red velvet ribbon; metallic thread; white glue; artificial cherries with leaves.

Directions:

1. Using the craft knife and the cookie cutters as patterns, cut out as many ornaments from the balsa wood as desired. Sand the edges of each shape smooth. Cut a small hole about ½ inch from the top of each ornament.

2. Paint all the shapes white on one side and let the paint dry completely. Turn over the ornaments, and paint the other side and the edges white. Let the paint dry completely.

3. When the white paint has dried, carefully place pieces of the tape on the shape to form stripes. Try to space the stripes evenly. Paint the stripes without tape red. Let the paint dry, turn over the shape and repeat the taping and painting on the opposite side. Paint the edges of each ornament to match the red and white striping on the front and back sides.

4. For each ornament, cut a length of red velvet ribbon and tie the ribbon into a bow. Glue a double cherry with leaves on top of the bow and let the glue dry. Glue the bow and cherries to the top of the ornament directly above the hole.

5. Cut a longer length of gold metallic thread. Insert one end of the thread through the hole in the top of the ornament. Wrap the thread around the bow with the cherries. Repeat two times to further secure the bow and cherries to the ornament. Knot the ends of the thread to make a hanger.

TIPS FOR A "GREEN" CHRISTMAS

Giving Back

At holiday time, it is important to remember those in need with donations of clothing and usable household goods. Putting useful items that you no longer need back into circulation not only is valuable in terms of recycling, it also can help bring back the spirit of giving into your Christmas celebration. Get the whole family to make up a care package of clothes, dishware, appliances, toys — even books and records. Call the Salvation Army, Goodwill Industries or charitable organization of choice for a drop location near you.

O TANNENBAUM TREE SKIRT

Average: For those with some experience in stenciling and quilting.

Materials: 1¼ yards of 45-inch-wide bleached muslin; 1½ yards of red calico fabric; 1¼ yards of 45-inch-wide synthetic batting; red sewing thread; white quilting thread; Stencil-Ease® "New England Bows" and "Christmas Designs" stencils; Fab-Tex™ fabric stenciling paints: Dark Red, Bright Green, and Colonial Golde; three No. 10 or 12 stencil brushes; between needle *(optional)*; quilting hoop *(optional)*; washable fabric marker; measuring tape; thumbtack; string; yardstick; masking tape; paper toweling; paper; iron; newspaper *(optional)*; cotton rags *(optional)*; rubbing alcohol *(optional)*.

Directions:

1. Wash and iron the fabrics. Tape the muslin square to a flat surface. Locate the center of the muslin, and use the thumbtack to secure one end of the string to the center. Attach the fabric marker to the other end of the string, positioning the marker at the edge of the muslin. Keeping the string taut, swing the marker around to mark a 45-inch-diameter circle. Shorten the string to 4½ inches, and mark a 9-inch-diameter circle in the center of the muslin. Draw a straight line from the smaller to the larger circle for the skirt opening.

2. Place the skirt on a hard surface. Place several layers of paper toweling underneath the skirt where you will start stenciling. Dampen a piece of paper toweling with water. Wipe the bristles of a stencil brush across the damp paper to pick up a slight amount of moisture on the bristles. Following Winter Village Stenciled Tablecloth & Napkins, Step 4 *(page 41)*, and using the photo as a color

guide, stencil a bow on one side of the skirt opening 4¼ inches from the outer edge of the skirt. Stencil nine more bows evenly spaced around the outer edge. Retape the stencil to block off the bow, and stencil a rope swag between each bow, adjusting the stencil as necessary. Stencil a Christmas tree above and a bell below each bow. Stencil poinsettias around the center of the skirt, leaving a ½-inch seam allowance. Clean the stencils and brushes following Winter Village Stenciled Tablecloth & Napkins, Step 6.

3. Let the stenciled skirt dry overnight. Set an iron on dry and press directly over each stenciled area for 25 to 30 seconds.

4. Cut out the stenciled skirt on the marked lines. Using the skirt as a pattern, cut the batting and a calico skirt back to the same size. Place the calico back on the stenciled skirt, right sides together, and the batting on top of the calico. Stitch all the layers together ½ inch from the edges, leaving one straight edge open. Turn the skirt right side out and slipstitch the open edge closed *(see Stitch Guide, page 168)*.

5. If hand-quilting, place the skirt in the hoop. Using the between needle and quilting thread, quilt a line around the stenciled trees and swags *(see Stitch Guide)*. Repeat 1 inch inside the first line three times *(see photo)*. Or quilt by machine.

6. Make bias binding, pieced as needed, from the remaining calico. Leaving enough binding extending beyond the skirt opening edges for ties, sew the binding to the front center edge of the skirt using a ½-inch seam *(see photo)*. Turn the binding to the back, and slipstitch the binding to the skirt back *(see Stitch Guide)*. Turn in the ties' raw edges. Slipstitch each tie closed along its long edge and short end.

CHRISTMAS KITCHEN CHANDELIER
(12 inches in diameter)

Average: For those with some experience in crafting.

Materials: 12-inch-diameter grapevine wreath; cookie cutters: 2 each of star, heart, gingerbread man, bell and Christmas tree, or shapes desired; ten ¼-inch-diameter red candles; 13 yards of 1-inch-wide red, green and white checked ribbon; 2 yards of 1-inch-wide red grosgrain ribbon; 2¼ yards of ⅛-inch-wide red grosgrain ribbon; 1 yard of ⅛-inch-wide gold cording; gold glitter; artificial bird; 10 stems each of artificial holly and mistletoe; sphagnum moss; floral wire; red wide felt tip marker; plastic coffee can lid; white craft glue; hot glue gun, or thick craft glue.

Directions:

1. Cut off the candle bottoms so the candles are 2 inches long. Dip the wicks into the white glue, and then into the glitter. Let the glue dry.

2. Wrap gold cording twice around the base of each candle. Cut the cording, and glue it to the base.

3. Using the glue gun or thick glue, glue a candle to the inside bottom of each cookie cutter *(see photo)*.

4. Cut the checked ribbon into ten 46-inch lengths. Thread about 4 inches of one ribbon length through the top of a cookie cutter. Make a single knot, and trim the short end of the ribbon to 1 inch. Repeat with the remaining ribbon lengths and cookie cutters.

5. Cut ten 8-inch lengths of ⅛-inch-wide grosgrain ribbon. Wrap a length above each checked ribbon knot, and tie the ends in a bow.

6. Separate the moss, and cover the wreath completely with it. Place the wreath on a flat surface. Leaving the cookie cutter and about 12 inches of ribbon hanging below the wreath, wrap the long end of one checked ribbon around the wreath from the outside over the top to the inside, under the bottom to the outside, and up to the top again. Repeat with the remaining checked ribbons, varying the lengths of the cookie cutter ends and spacing the ribbons evenly around the wreath *(see photo)*.

7. Gather the checked ribbons' short ends above the wreath; the ribbons' lengths will be uneven. Make sure the ribbons' edges are even and straight. Starting 14 inches above the wreath, wrap about 5 inches of floral wire around the ribbons. Leave 3 inches of the ribbon ends free at the top, and cut off the excess ribbon.

8. Cut a 1½-inch-diameter circle from the plastic coffee can lid. Color the circle with the red marker. Cut an X in the center of the circle, and insert the free ends of the checked ribbons through the opening. Secure the ribbon ends above the plastic circle by wrapping them with wire.

9. Wrap a length of 1-inch-wide grosgrain ribbon around the wire above the circle. Glue the grosgrain ribbon in place, securing the ends. Cut another length of 1-inch-wide grosgrain ribbon, and fold it in half to make a loop for a hanger. Glue and wire the hanger ends to the top of the chandelier just above the plastic circle. Make a bow with the remaining 1-inch-wide grosgrain ribbon, and attach it to the top of the chandelier to cover the hanger ends.

10. Decorate the wreath with the holly, mistletoe and bird *(see photo)*.

TIPS FOR A "GREEN" CHRISTMAS

Environment-Smart Sparkle

When you want to give your Christmas tree extra sparkle, you probably trim it with tinsel, then throw the tinsel away. Besides producing waste, most places that recycle Christmas trees won't accept any with tinsel on them. But there are alternatives to add glitter without waste.

- Strings of sequins. Use these as garlands, or cut the strings into smaller strips and hang the strips from branches to look like icicles.
- Metallic ribbons. Either tie the ribbons in bows and wire them to branches, or curl lengths of ribbons and use them as streamers.
- Strings of faceted beads, gold or silver beads, or fake pearls.
- Tiny mirrors. Hang them like ornaments.
- Glass ball ornaments. To add extra sparkle, spray glue on the balls and roll them in glitter, or glue sequins to the balls in a pleasing design.
- Tin or metallic paper ornaments.
- Chandelier crystals.

GIFTS OF NATURE KISSING BALL

All the natural trims you need for this lovely ornament can be found on a walk through the autumn woods.

Easy: Achievable by anyone.

Materials: 6- to 8-inch diameter Styrofoam® ball, or large ball ornament; tiny pine cones; acorns; gumballs; nuts; 1-inch-wide metallic gold ribbon; hot glue gun.

Directions:
Glue the pine cones, acorns, gumballs and nuts to the Styrofoam ball or large ball ornament to cover it completely. Glue a ribbon loop to the top of the ball for a hanger.

RIBBON PATCHWORK STOCKING

(photo, pages 62-63)

Average: For those with some experience in sewing.

Materials: ½ yard of solid color fabric; ¼ yard each of assorted ribbons, laces, eyelet laces, cluny laces and fringes in various widths; extra-wide double fold bias tape; matching threads; purchased appliqué; assorted fabric scraps; synthetic batting; 4 buttons; sewing needle; paper for pattern.

Directions:
(¼-inch seams allowed):
1. Using the photo on pages 62-63 as a guide, draw a stocking pattern on paper. Add a ¼-inch seam allowance to all but the top edge. Cut out four stockings from the solid color fabric, and two stockings from the batting.
2. Arrange the fabric scraps and appliqué on the right side of one fabric stocking. Cover the scraps' raw edges with the assorted trims. Sew the buttons to a wide ribbon *(see photo)*. Topstitch the trims in place.
3. Place a fabric stocking wrong side up. Place a batting stocking and then the patchwork stocking, right side up, on top. Stitch the stockings together along the outside edges to make the stocking front. Repeat with the remaining batting and fabric stockings for the stocking back.
4. Stitch the stocking front and back right sides together, leaving the top edge open. Turn the stocking right side out. Starting at the back seam and with raw edges even, stitch one long edge of the bias tape to the stocking top edge. Leaving enough tape at the back seam for a hanger, fold the tape to the inside of the stocking and slipstitch it in place *(see Stitch Guide, page 168)*. Make a loop for a hanger with the extra tape, and stitch the hanger to the inside back seam.

WHITE QUILTED STOCKING

(photo, pages 62-63)

Average: For those with some experience in sewing.

Materials: ½ yard of quilted satin fabric; ½ yard of lining fabric; matching threads; 2½ yards of ³⁄₁₆-inch-wide lurex-edge velvet ribbon; 2¼ yards of ³⁄₈-inch-wide metallic grosgrain ribbon; ½ yard of synthetic batting; white glue; paper for pattern.
Directions:
1. Using the photo on pages 62-63 as a guide, draw a stocking pattern on paper. Cut out two stockings from the batting. Add a ⁵⁄₈-inch seam allowance to the pattern, and cut out two stockings each from the quilted fabric and lining.
2. Using the photo as a placement guide, glue lengths of the velvet and metallic ribbons to the right side of each quilted stocking.
3. Working from the right side, pin a batting stocking to the wrong side of each quilted stocking. Stitch the quilted stockings right sides together, leaving the top edge open. Clip the curves, and turn the stocking right side out. Do not remove the pins yet.
4. Stitch the lining stockings together the same way, but do not turn them. Slip the lining into the quilted stocking. Turn in the stocking and lining seam allowances at the top edge, and pin them in place. Fold a 6-inch length of metallic ribbon into a loop, and tack the loop ends together. Slip the loop ends between the lining and stocking at the stocking's back seam, and tack the loop in place for a hanger. Slipstitch the stocking and lining together, reinforcing the hanger while stitching *(see Stitch Guide, page 168)*. Remove the pins.

SAMPLER STOCKING

(photo, pages 62-63)

Average: For those with some experience in sewing and counted cross stitch.

Materials: 23 x 12 inches of 6-mesh natural burlap; 23 x 12 inches of fabric for stocking back; two 23 x 12-inch pieces of lining fabric; matching threads; 4-ply worsted knitting yarn: 20 yards of Red, 12 yards of Green, 3 yards of Brown, 1 yard of Yellow, and ½ yard of Blue; tapestry needle; embroidery hoop.
Directions:
1. The stocking is 19½ inches long from top to bottom. Using this dimension, and those marked on the chart in Fig. III, 5, pencil an outline of the stocking on the burlap. Staystitch the edges of the burlap by machine to prevent raveling.
2. The Red cross stitches at the top and bottom of the stocking are worked over 3 threads. The cross stitches for the design in Fig. III, 5 are worked over 2 threads. Place the burlap in the embroidery hoop. Using the yarn and tapestry needle, work eight rows of Red cross stitches across the top of the stocking, and four rows of cross stitches across the bottom of the stocking *(see Stitch Guide, page 168)*. Then cross stitch the design in Fig. III, 5 on the stocking; each symbol in Fig. III, 5 represents one cross stitch worked over 2 threads in the color indicated.
3. When the cross stitching is completed, baste around the stocking outline. Press the embroidered burlap, right side down, with a damp cloth to block it. Let the burlap dry.
4. With right sides together, stitch the embroidered burlap to the stocking back fabric over the basted outline, leaving the top edge open. Trim all edges to a ½-inch seam allowance.

5. Cut two stockings from the lining fabric to match the embroidered stocking, including the seam allowance. Stitch the lining stockings, right sides together, leaving the top edge and toe open.

6. Twist together four 10-inch lengths of Red yarn. Repeat. Wind the twisted yarns together in the opposite direction to make a cord. Fold the cord into a loop, and tack it to the top of the embroidered stocking's back seam for a hanger.

7. Clip the curves, and turn the stocking right side out. Do not turn the lining. Insert the stocking into the lining. Stitch the top of the stocking to the top of the lining. Pull out the stocking through the toe of the lining. Turn in the open toe edges, and slipstitch the opening closed *(see Stitch Guide)*. Insert the lining into the stocking and take a few stitches to secure it in place. Press the finished stocking lightly.

FIG. III, 5   SAMPLER STOCKING

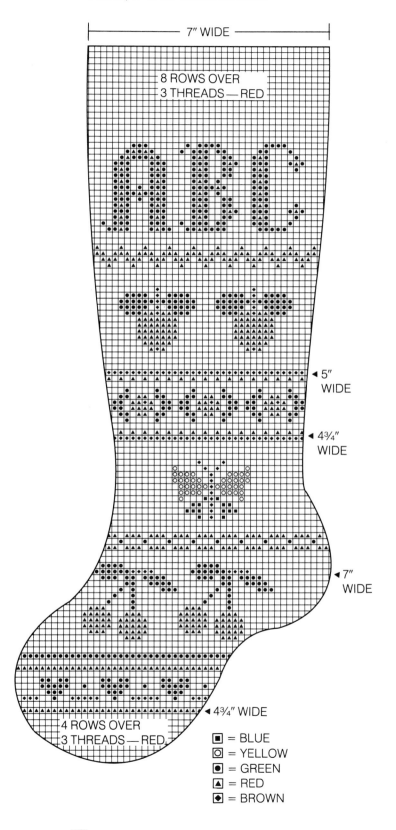

7" WIDE

8 ROWS OVER
3 THREADS — RED

◄ 5" WIDE

◄ 4¾" WIDE

◄ 7" WIDE

◄ 4¾" WIDE

4 ROWS OVER
3 THREADS — RED

■ = BLUE
◙ = YELLOW
◉ = GREEN
▲ = RED
◆ = BROWN

CHECKED STOCKING

(photo, pages 62-63)

Average: For those with some experience in knitting.

Materials: Aunt Lydia's Rug Yarn: 2 skeins of Emerald Green, and 1 skein each of White, Red and Gold; four size 10½ double-pointed knitting needles (dp); size G crochet hook.
Note: *Carry the unused colors loosely on the wrong side of the work. If you wish, twist the unused colors with the working yarn every 2 sts.*
Directions:
1. Stocking: With Emerald Green, cast on 56 sts, dividing them evenly among 3 dp needles. Close the circle, and k 2 rows. **Check Pattern, Rows 1 to 4:** *K 4 Green, k 4 Gold; rep from * around. **Rows 5 to 8:** *K 4 Red, k 4 Green; rep from * around. **Rows 9 to 12:** *K 4 Green, k 4 White; rep from * around. **Rows 13 to 16:** Rep Rows 1 to 4. Repeat Rows 5 to 16 twice. Drop all colors but Green. Work one row in Green.
2. Heel: K 14 sts on 1 dp needle, k 28 sts on 2nd dp needle, k 14 sts on 3rd needle and slip the first 14 sts onto the 3rd needle. Break off the

yarn. Work only the 28 sts on the 2nd needle for the Heel. Join Green. Work 2 inches of k 1, p 1 ribbing; end on the right side. **Row 1 (wrong side):** P 16, p 2 tog, p 1, turn; sl 1, k 7, sl 1, k 1, psso, k 1, turn; sl 1, k 5, sl 1, k 1, psso, k 1, turn; sl 1, p 6, p 2 tog, p 1, turn; sl 1, p 8, p 2 tog, p 1, turn. Continue in this way, working 1 more stitch on each row until all sts have been worked. End on the right side with 16 sts. Pick up and k 4 sts along the side of the Heel. On the 2nd needle, k across 28 sts of the instep. On the 3rd needle, pick up 4 sts along the side of the Heel and k 8 sts across the Heel. There should be 12 sts on each Heel needle.
3. Shaping, Rnd 1: On the 1st needle, k 9, k 2 tog, k 1; on the 2nd needle, k 28; on the 3rd needle, k 1, sl 1, k 1, psso, k 9. **Rnd 2:** K. Rep Rnds 1 and 2 until there are 6 sts on each Heel needle.
4. Foot: Work even for 4 inches. **Toe, Row 1:** K 2 tog, k 1; rep around. **Row 2:** K. **Row 3:** K 2 tog; rep around. Rep Rows 2 and 3. Draw the yarn through the rem sts, and fasten off from the wrong side. With the crochet hook, work 1 row of sc around the top of the Stocking in Red.

FROSTY THE SNOWMAN & JOLLY ST. NICK KNITTED STOCKINGS

(photo, pages 62-63)

Average: For those with some experience in knitting.

General Materials: Four size 6 double-pointed knitting needles (dp), OR ANY SIZE NEEDLES TO OBTAIN GAUGE BELOW; stitch holder; crewel needle.
Gauge: 5 sts = 1 inch; 6 rows = 1 inch.
General Directions:
1. Stocking: With MC, cast on 64 sts, dividing them among 3 dp needles 22-21-21. Close the circle. **Rows 1 to 18:** P each row. **Rows 19 to 38:** K each row. **Row 39:** Dec 1 st at beg of each needle (61 sts). Rep Rows 19 to 39 three times (52 sts). K next row.
2. Heel: Divide the sts between 2 needles. Slip 26 sts onto the stitch holder, and work the remaining 26 sts. **Rows 1 to 26:** K each row. **Row 27:** K 13, sl 1, k 1, psso, k 1, turn. **Row 28:** P 2, p 2 tog, p 1, turn. **Row 29:** K 4, sl 1, k 1, psso, k 1, turn. **Row 30:** P 6, p 2 tog, p 1, turn. Continue this way until 1 st remains after the space. K tog with the next st. P across until last 2 sts, p 2 tog (16 sts). Break off the yarn.
3. Shaping: With the right side facing, tie the yarn at the beginning of the top of the Heel; pick up and k 13 sts. Work across 16 sts on the Heel needle. Pick up and k 13 sts on the other side of the Heel. Divide the 42 sts between the 2 needles. K and return the 26 sts on the stitch holder to the third needle. **Rows 1 to 7:** K each row, dec 1 st at the beginning of the first Heel needle and the end of the second Heel needle (54 sts). **Rows 8 to 36:** K each row.
4. Toe, Row 1: K 1 row, dec 1 st at the beginning of the first Heel needle

and at the end of the second Heel needle. **Row 2:** Dec 1 st at each end of the front needle, at the beginning of the first Heel needle and at the end of the second Heel needle. **Row 3:** K 1 row. Rep Rows 2 and 3 seven times (20 sts). Place 10 sts on each of 2 needles. Weave the Toe with the crewel needle, and run the end of the yarn into the knitting.

5. Top Trim: With White, cast on 65 sts. K 3 rows. Bind off.

6. Hanger: With MC, cast on 30 sts. K 3 rows. Bind off.

7. Figure: Make Frosty the Snowman or Jolly St. Nick following the individual directions below.

8. Finishing: Press all knitted pieces with a warm steam iron. Using the crewel needle and matching yarn, sew the Top Trim to the Stocking, joining the Trim's ends at the back. Fold the Hanger into a loop, and sew it to the inside back of the stocking. Attach Frosty the Snowman or Jolly St. Nick to the Stocking following the individual directions.

FROSTY THE SNOWMAN STOCKING

Materials: Lion Brand Pamela 4-ply knitting worsted yarn (3½-ounce skein): 1 skein of Scarlet (MC), and small amounts of White, Orange, Emerald and Black; General Materials.

Directions:

1. Make the Stocking following General Directions, Steps 1 to 6.

2. Snowman: With White, cast on 13 sts. **Rows 1 to 3:** K each row. **Row 4:** Inc 1 st each side (15 sts). **Rows 5 to 13:** K each row. **Row 14:** Inc 1 st each side. **Rows 15 to 21:** K each row. **Row 22:** Dec 1 st each side. **Rows 23 and 24:** K each row. **Row 25:** Dec 1 st each side. **Row 26:** K 1 row. **Row**

27: Inc 1 st each side. **Rows 28 to 38:** K each row. **Row 39:** Dec 1 st each side. **Row 40:** K 1 row. **Rows 41 and 42:** Dec 1 st each side. **Row 43:** K 1 row. **Row 44:** Inc 1 st each side. **Rows 45 to 48:** K each row. **Row 49:** Inc 1 st each side. **Rows 50 to 57:** K each row. Bind off.

3. Scarf: With Emerald, cast on 4 sts. K 14 rows. Bind off.

4. Scarf Ends: With Emerald, cast on 4 sts, k 15 rows, and bind off for 1 scarf end. With Emerald, cast on 4 sts, k 13 rows, and bind off for the other scarf end.

5. Button/Eye (make 5): With Black, cast on 4 sts. **Row 1:** K 1 row. **Row 2:** P 1 row. Gather the edges of the knitted strip, and add a few Black yarn scraps inside. Pull the gathered strip into a ball, and tie it.

6. Hat: With Black, cast on 11 sts. **Row 1:** K 1 row. **Row 2:** P 1 row. Rep Rows 1 and 2 six times. Bind off.

7. Hat Brim: With Black, cast on 18 sts. K 1 row. Bind off.

8. Nose: With Orange, cast on 3 sts. **Row 1:** K 1 row. **Row 2:** P 1 row. Bind off. Sew the knitted strip into a carrot shape.

9. Finishing: Press all knitted pieces and finish the Stocking following General Directions, Step 8. Using the crewel needle and matching yarn, sew the Snowman to the center of the Stocking. Sew the Hat and Hat Brim in place. Sew 2 Eyes and the Nose to the Snowman. Make the mouth with 2-ply Scarlet yarn. Sew 3 Buttons down the Snowman's front. Sew the Scarf and Scarf Ends around the neck *(see photo, pages 62-63)*.

JOLLY ST. NICK STOCKING

Materials: Lion Brand Pamela 4-ply knitting worsted yarn (3½-ounce skein): 1 skein of Emerald (MC), and small amounts of White, Light Pink and Scarlet; two ⅜-inch-diameter blue shank buttons; General Materials.

Directions:

1. Stocking: Make the Stocking following General Directions, Steps 1 to 6.

2. Face: With Light Pink, cast on 15 sts. **Row 1:** K 1 row. **Row 2:** P 1 row. Rep Rows 1 and 2 eight times. Bind off.

3. Nose: With Light Pink, cast on 4 sts. **Row 1:** K 1 row. **Row 2:** P 1 row. Rep Rows 1 and 2 twice. Bind off. Gather the edges of the knitted strip, and add a few Light Pink yarn scraps inside. Pull the strip into a ball, and tie it.

4. Beard: With White, cast on 15 sts. **Rows 1 to 4:** K each row. **Row 5:** K 1 row, inc 1 st each side. **Rows 6 to 20:** K each row. **Row 21:** K 3 sts; bind off the middle 11 sts; slip the last 3 sts onto the stitch holder. **Rows 22 to 35:** K each row. Bind off. Pick up the 3 sts on the stitch holder, and k 14 rows. Bind off.

5. Cap: With White, cast on 17 sts. **Rows 1 to 4:** K each row. Change to Scarlet. **Row 5:** K 1 row. **Row 6:** P 1 row. **Row 7:** K 1 row, dec 1 st each side. **Row 8:** P 1 row. **Row 9:** K 1 row. **Row 10:** P 1 row. **Row 11:** K 1 row, dec 1 st each side. Rep Rows 8 to 11 six times. K 1 row. P 5 rows on the remaining 5 sts. Bind off.

6. Pompon: With White, cast on 9 sts. Knit 12 rows. Bind off. Gather the edges of the knitted strip, and add a few White yarn scraps inside. Pull the gathered strip into a ball, and tie it.

7. Finishing: Press all knitted pieces and finish the Stocking following General Directions, Step 8. Using the crewel needle and matching yarn, sew the Face to the Stocking. Sew the Beard over the Face. Sew the Cap over the top of the Face, leaving the Cap tip loose. Sew the Pompon to the tip of the Cap. Sew the blue buttons to the Face for eyes. Using 2-ply White yarn, make a few stitches over the eyes for eyebrows *(see photo, pages 62-63)*. Sew the Nose in place. Make the mouth with 2-ply Scarlet yarn.

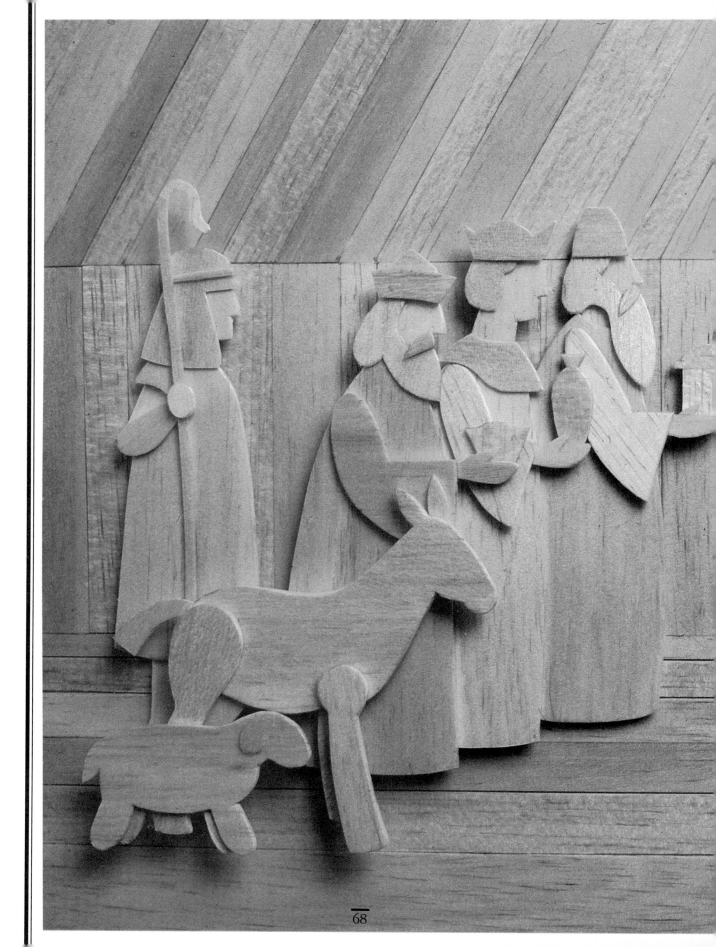

BALSA WOOD NATIVITY SCENE

(photo, pages 68-69)
The beauty of the crèche recreated in balsa wood. The layering of the wood pieces gives this lovely project its three-dimensional quality.

Average: For those with some experience in woodworking.

Materials: 3 x 36-inch balsa wood planks: one 1/32 inch thick, two 1/16 inch thick, and three 1/8 inch thick; two 16½ x 11-inch illustration boards; graphite paper; stylus or dry ballpoint pen; sandpaper; tack cloth; clear varnish; 1-inch foam brushes; straight edge metal ruler; utility knife; craft knife with No. 11 blade; white craft glue; newspapers; sawtooth hanger *(optional)*; tracing paper for patterns.

Directions:

1. Manger Window: The photo *(pages 68-69)* is the actual size of the project, and can be used as the pattern for the manger and all the figures. Using the photo as the pattern, trace the location and shape of the manger window opening onto tracing paper. Cover a flat surface with a thickness of newspapers, and place one illustration board on it. Using graphite paper and the stylus or dry ballpoint pen, transfer the window opening to the illustration board. Cut out the window opening with the utility knife. Place the board with the window opening on top of the remaining illustration board, and mark the window opening on the second background board.

2. Window Scene: Cut a 4½-inch length from the 1/32-inch-thick balsa plank. Glue the length to the upper part of background board's marked window opening as the sky that is seen through the window. Cut several curved lengths from the 1/16-inch-thick balsa as hills. Using the photo as a placement guide, glue the hills to the wood sky piece and the background board to fill in the remaining space in the window opening.

3. Manger Floor, Wall and Window Frame: Using the straight edge ruler and utility knife, and the photo as the pattern, measure and cut the pieces for the manger floor, wall, and window frame from the 1/8-inch-thick balsa; the manger wall and floor extend ½ inch beyond the photo's top, bottom and sides. Glue the floor and wall pieces flush with the window opening. Glue the window frame around the window opening over the wall pieces.

4. Cutting the Figures: Using the photo as the pattern, trace each piece of each figure separately onto tracing paper, filling in the lines of any covered edges. Using the graphite paper and stylus or dry ballpoint pen, transfer each figure piece to the balsa indicated. Cut out each figure piece with the craft knife. Keep all the pieces for each figure together.

5. Mary: From the 1/16-inch-thick balsa, cut out the head and left sleeve as one piece, the body, and the left hand. From the 1/32-inch-thick balsa, cut out the veil.

6. Joseph: From the 1/16-inch-thick balsa, cut out the head and robe as one piece, the left sleeve, and the left hand. From the 1/32-inch-thick balsa, cut out the beard, moustache, headcloth, and headband.

7. Christ Child and Crib: From the 1/16-inch-thick balsa, cut out the head, halo, crib rim, four horizontal crib pieces, and four crib legs.

8. Three Wise Men: For the wise men on the left and in the middle, cut out the head and robe as one piece, the right sleeve, right hand, and gift from the 1/16-inch-thick balsa. Repeat for the wise man on the right, but make the head and robe separate pieces. Also cut the collar for the wise man in the middle from the 1/16-inch-thick balsa. From the 1/32-inch-thick balsa, cut out the hair/beards, moustaches, and crowns.

9. Shepherd on the Left: From the 1/16-inch-thick balsa, cut out the head and tunic as one piece, the upper right arm, lower right arm, right hand, and two legs. From the 1/32-inch-thick balsa, cut out the crook, headcloth, and headband.

10. Shepherd on the Right: From the 1/16-inch-thick balsa, cut out the head and robe as one piece, the left sleeve, and the left hand. From the 1/32-inch-thick balsa, cut out the beard, headcloth, headband, and moustache.

11. Shepherd Boy: From the 1/16-inch-thick balsa, cut out the head and tunic as one piece, the left, and the left arm. From the 1/32-inch-thick balsa, cut out the headcloth and headband.

12. Sheep: The body piece includes the head, tail, and two legs. For each sheep, cut out the body piece, the ear, and the two partially hidden legs from the 1/16-inch-thick balsa.

13. Donkey: The body piece includes the head, right ear, and tail. From the 1/16-inch-thick balsa, cut out the body piece, left ear, and four legs.

14. Assembling the Figures: When all the pieces for each figure have been cut out, sand their edges lightly to round the edges and remove any roughness. Wipe off all the sawdust with the tack cloth. Using the foam brushes, varnish the manger floor, wall, window frame, window scene, and the pieces for each figure. Let the varnish dry completely. Using the craft glue, assemble each figure. Let the glue dry completely.

15. Attaching the Figures: Using the photo as a placement guide, arrange the figures on the manger wall. Glue Mary and Joseph together where they overlap, and glue the pair to the manger wall. Glue the wise men together where they overlap. Cut four 1 x 4-inch lengths from the 1/16-inch-thick balsa for supports. Glue two of the supports together. Glue the double-thickness support to the center back of the wise man on the left. Glue a single-thickness support to the back of the wise man in the middle. Glue the remaining single-thickness support to the back of the shepherd on the left. Glue the wise men and shepherd on the left to the manger wall. Cut another double-thickness support, and glue it to the back of the shepherd on the right. Glue the shepherd boy to him, and glue the pair to the manger wall. Glue the left-facing sheep to the shepherd boy. Glue the right-facing sheep to the donkey. Cut and glue a 2 x 1-inch double-thickness support to the back of the donkey. Glue the donkey to the wise man on the left. Glue the Child to the crib. Cut and glue a 1 x 1-inch support to the crib's left side on the back. Glue the crib to Mary. Let the glue dry completely.

16. Completing the Manger: Cut one 12-inch, two 10-inch, and one 8-inch length from the 1/8-inch-thick balsa. Glue a 10-inch length to each side of the background board. Glue the 12-inch length to the bottom, and the 8-inch length to the top left of the background board. Let the glue dry completely. Place the manger board over the background board, outer edges flush, and glue the boards together along the wood strips. If you wish, make a thin frame from the 1/8-inch-thick balsa, and glue the frame to the manger's outside edges. If you wish to hang the nativity scene, glue a sawtooth hanger to the back.

ORNAMENTS TO TREASURE

Make any or all of these festive ornaments
to delight young and old. Celebrate the
season with a bevy of St. Nick ornaments.
Or give a country-style look to your tree
with balsa wood ornaments.

PAPER SANTA ORNAMENT

Easy: Achievable by anyone.

Materials: 1 sheet each of pink, white and red construction paper; 1½-inch-diameter cardboard tube; metallic gold thread; craft knife; scissors; ruler; pins; rubber cement; pencil; manila folder, or other lightweight cardboard, for pattern.

Note: *It is easier to cut the construction paper with the craft knife and ruler than with scissors. When covering the cardboard tube with the construction paper, keep the overlapping ends of the paper in a vertical line at the back of the ornament unless otherwise noted. If necessary, pin the paper pieces in place until the glue sets.*

Directions:

1. Cut a 4-inch length of cardboard tube. Cover the outer side and one open end of the tube with red paper; the uncovered end is the bottom of the ornament.

2. Cut a 1-inch-wide pink paper strip. Glue the strip around the tube, with the strip's bottom edge 2¼ inches above the ornament's bottom edge.

3. Enlarge the Hat pattern in Fɪɢ. III, 6 onto the manila folder or other lightweight cardboard, following the directions on page 169. Cut out the manila pattern. Enlarge the Beard half-pattern onto folded manila, cut the folded manila around the outside pattern lines, and open the manila for the full pattern.

4. Cut a Hat from red paper. Glue the Hat around the tube, with the Hat's bottom edge 3¼ inches above the ornament's bottom edge, and the Hat's overlapping edges above the ornament's left ear *(see photo)*. Cut a ½-inch-wide white paper strip for a hatband. Glue the hatband around the ornament, with the hatband's bottom edge 2⅞ inches above the ornament's bottom edge. Bend the tip of the Hat over to the opposite side of the ornament, and glue the tip in place *(see photo)*. Cut a ⅜-inch-wide white paper strip, and roll it around the pencil. Glue the roll to the tip of the Hat for a pompon.

5. Cut a Beard from white paper, and cut along the marked pattern lines to make fringes. Curl the end of each fringe and each Beard side strip by running it over a sharp scissor edge. Glue the Beard to the face. Extend the Beard fringes in varying lengths *(see photo)*, and hold each fringe in place with a dab of glue.

6. Cut and roll a ½-inch-wide pink paper strip for a nose. Glue the nose in place. Run a length of gold thread through the top of the Hat, and tie the thread ends to make a hanger loop.

CLEVER CRAFTING

The Cutting Edge

A craft knife is an indispensable tool when you're working with cardboard, balsa wood or paper, but the knife should be used carefully!

● Always cut on a padded surface, such as an old magazine, a piece of cardboard, or several layers of newspaper.

● Cut in a slow, smooth motion to avoid creating bumps or rough edges. When you're cutting thick material, score it first by cutting a slight indentation along the entire cutting edge before slicing through. To cut a straight edge, hold a ruler firmly along the cutting edge, and keep the knife blade against the ruler while you cut.

● Keep the open blade away from curious youngsters. Store the craft knife in a tool kit or other closed box where kids can't get to it.

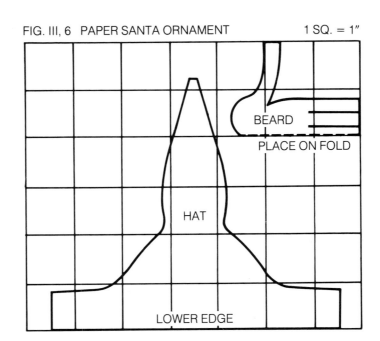

FIG. III, 6 PAPER SANTA ORNAMENT   1 SQ. = 1"

BEARD

PLACE ON FOLD

HAT

LOWER EDGE

PEEK-A-BOO SANTA

Easy: Achievable by anyone.

Materials: 31 x 24-mesh plastic canvas rectangle; felt for ornament back; 3-ply tapestry yarn: White, Peach, Bright Red, Brick Red, Blue, Black, and Golden Brown; tapestry needle; ½-inch-diameter white pompon; glue.

Directions:

1. Using three strands of yarn in the needle, and following the chart in Fig. III, 7 for stitch placement and colors, work the bricks in continental stitch over two meshes. Fill in the corners, and work the rest of the ornament except the eyes, in continental stitch over one mesh. Work each eye in Blue smyrna stitch. Work a single strand Black French knot in the center of each eye. Outline the bricks in single strand Black straight stitch *(see Stitch Guide, page 168).*

2. When the embroidering is complete, cut out the ornament *(see Fig. III, 7).* Using the embroidered ornament as a pattern, cut a felt ornament back.

3. Using corresponding color yarn, whipstitch around the edges of the ornament *(see Stitch Guide).* Glue the pompon to the top of the hat. Glue the felt back to the ornament, catching in the ends of a length of yarn to make a loop for a hanger.

CLEVER CRAFTING

Kid-Proof Hangers

If you have toddlers, or are making ornaments for folks who have small children, use yarn or ribbon to make hanger loops. Soft hangers are safer than metal hooks or metallic threads when inquisitive little ones are around.

FIG. III, 7 PEEK-A-BOO SANTA

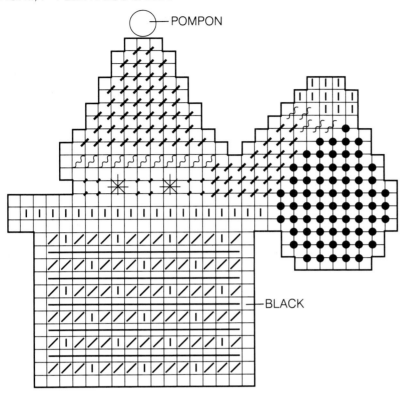

POMPON

BLACK

☑ = BRICK RED
☑ = WHITE
☑ = PEACH
✳ = BLUE
☑ = BRIGHT RED
◉ = GOLDEN BROWN

CLEVER CRAFTING

Canvas with a Twist

Plastic canvas is a great material for needlepoint beginners to use. It's easy to handle and doesn't distort, even when stitch tension isn't entirely even. Plus, the large holes make it easy and fast to finish a stitched piece.

If you've got budding young crafters at home, let them try stitching plastic canvas ornaments of their own.

SANTA SACK
(6½ x 5 inches)

Easy: Achievable by anyone.

Materials: Two 7¾ x 6-inch rectangles of loose-weave white fabric, or cut from dishcloth; matching thread; felt: 3 x 4 inches of white, 2½ x 3 inches of red, 1½ x 1¼ inches of pale pink, and 1 square inch of dark pink; 16 inches of ⅛-inch-wide red ribbon; ½-inch-diameter white pompon; ¼-inch-diameter red pompon; two ¼-inch-diameter plastic eyes; glue.

Directions (½-inch seams allowed):

1. Sack: Stitch the white fabric or dishcloth rectangles, right sides together, along the long edges and one short end. Turn the sack right side out. Turn the open edges to the wrong side, and stitch a ½-inch casing. Insert the ribbon in the casing, and tie the ribbon ends together.

2. Santa: Cut 1 inch off the white felt to make a 3-inch square and a 1 x 3-inch rectangle. Cut two 1-inch-wide, 1½-inch-long curved moustaches from the white rectangle. Cut a ½-inch square off each top corner of the white square. Beginning below the cut out squares, scallop three sides of the square to make a beard. Using the photo as a guide, cut out a 1 x ¾-inch face. Glue the pale pink felt to the white felt behind the face. Cut two ⅜-inch-diameter circles from the dark pink felt. Curve the edges of the red felt for the hat *(see photo)*.

3. Assembling: Glue the hat to the center of the sack. Glue the beard over the hat *(see photo)*. Glue the white pompon to the longer end of the hat. Glue the dark pink circles to the pale pink face. Glue the plastic eyes to the dark pink circles. Glue the moustaches just below the eyes *(see photo)*. Glue the red pompon over the moustaches for a nose.

SECRET SANTA
(6 x 3 inches)

Easy: Achievable by anyone.

Materials: Nylon stocking; 5 x 2½ inches of red ribbed top from anklet sock; 8 yards of 4-ply white yarn; matching threads; 2-inch square of green felt; 6 inches of ⅛-inch-wide green ribbon; 1-inch-diameter white pompon; ¼-inch-diameter red pompon; synthetic stuffing; tapestry needle; glue; paper for pattern.

Directions:

1. Cut 3½ inches off the nylon stocking toe to make a pouch. Stuff the pouch to make a 2-inch-wide, 2½-inch-long oval for a head. Gather the open top of the head, and tie it with thread. Pinch up a small ball of stuffing in the center of the head, and form a flat, ½-inch-diameter round nose. Wrap the nose with thread, and stitch to secure it.

2. Gather and stitch one end of the red sock top to form the peak of the cap *(see photo)*. Glue the center of the ribbon to the peak. Glue the white pompon over the ribbon. Tie the ribbon ends together to form a loop for a hanger.

3. Stuff the top half of the cap. Turn up the cap's lower edge ½ inch, and pull the cap down over the head *(see photo)*. Stitch the cap to the head through all layers.

4. Using the photo as a design guide, draw a holly leaf on paper. Using the paper pattern, cut out two holly leaves from the felt. Glue the holly leaves to the cap, along with the red pompon for a berry *(see photo)*.

5. Wind the white yarn around your thumb to cover 2 inches, slide the wound yarn off, and topstitch it by machine. Repeat until all the yarn is wound and stitched for the beard. Sew the beard to the face all around the bottom of the head *(see photo)*.

SANTA STOCKING
(6½ inches long)

Easy: Achievable by anyone.

Materials: Felt: 4½ x 6½ inches of red, and 2 x 4 inches of pink; thread; two ½-inch-diameter plastic eyes; 1½-inch-diameter white pompon; 1-inch-diameter red pompon; 11-inch giant-loop chenille; pinking shears; glue; paper for pattern.

Directions:

1. Cut a 4½ x 7-inch paper rectangle. Holding the rectangle so the short ends are at the top and bottom, cut off a 1½ x 4-inch strip from the upper left side. Round the bottom corners to create a stocking shape. Using the paper pattern and the pinking shears, cut two stockings from the red felt. Topstitch the stockings together ¼ inch from the raw edges, leaving the top edge open.

2. Glue the pink felt strip to the front of the stocking across the instep area for a face. Glue the plastic eyes to the face. Glue the red pompon to the face for a nose, and the chenille to the top and bottom of the face for hair and a beard. Glue the white pompon to the top right-hand corner of the stocking *(see photo)*.

TIPS FOR A "GREEN" CHRISTMAS

Ornamental Recycling

Don't throw away ball ornaments that are past their prime. Cover them with ribbons or sequins, paint them or decorate them with stickers.

For a fast, easy and beautiful "recycled" ornament, cut a square of fabric large enough to cover the ornament, plus about 1½ inches. Place the ornament in the center of the square, gather the edges of the square at the top and tie with yarn, twine or ribbon.

DANCING SANTA TREE TOPPER
(about 7½ inches tall)

Average: For those with some experience in woodworking.

Materials: Balsa wood: ⅟₃₂-, ⅟₁₆- and ³⁄₁₆-inch-thick planks, and ¼-inch-thick scrap; brass brads; scrap of brass wire; graphite paper; stylus or dry ballpoint pen; red and white flat paints; gold and black glossy paints; paintbrushes; craft knife; tack hammer; glue; paper for pattern.

Directions:

1. Trace the full-size pattern in FIG. III, 8 onto paper. Using the graphite paper and stylus or dry ballpoint pen, trace the Head/Hat, Left and Right Legs, Left and Right Arms, and Left and Right Boots onto the ⅟₁₆-inch-thick balsa. Trace the Body onto the ³⁄₁₆-inch-thick balsa. Trace the Pompon, Hatband, Nose, Moustache, Beard, Belt, Buckle, Suit Trim, two Sleeve Cuffs, and two Boot Cuffs onto the ⅟₃₂-inch-thick balsa. Cut out the wood pieces with the craft knife.

2. Using the photo and Head/Hat pattern as color guides, paint the front and sides of the wood pieces, mixing red and white paint to make pink paint. Let the paint dry completely.

3. Using the photo as a placement guide, glue the Pompon, Hatband, Beard, Moustache and Nose to the Head/Hat. Glue the Suit Trim, Belt and Buckle to the Body. Glue the Sleeve Cuffs to the Left and Right Arms, and the Boot Cuffs to the Left and Right Boots.

4. Nail two brass brads for eyes to the Head/Hat where indicated on the pattern. Using the photo as a placement guide, glue the Left Boot to the Left Leg, and the Head/Hat to the Body. Nail the Right Boot to the Right Leg, and both Legs and Arms to the Body where indicated on the pattern.

5. Glue the ¼-inch-thick balsa scrap to the back of the Left Leg, and push the brass wire into the scrap. Twist the extending end of the wire into a loop. Attach the Santa to the top of the tree with the loop.

FIG. III, 8 DANCING SANTA TREE TOPPER   FULL SIZE PATTERN

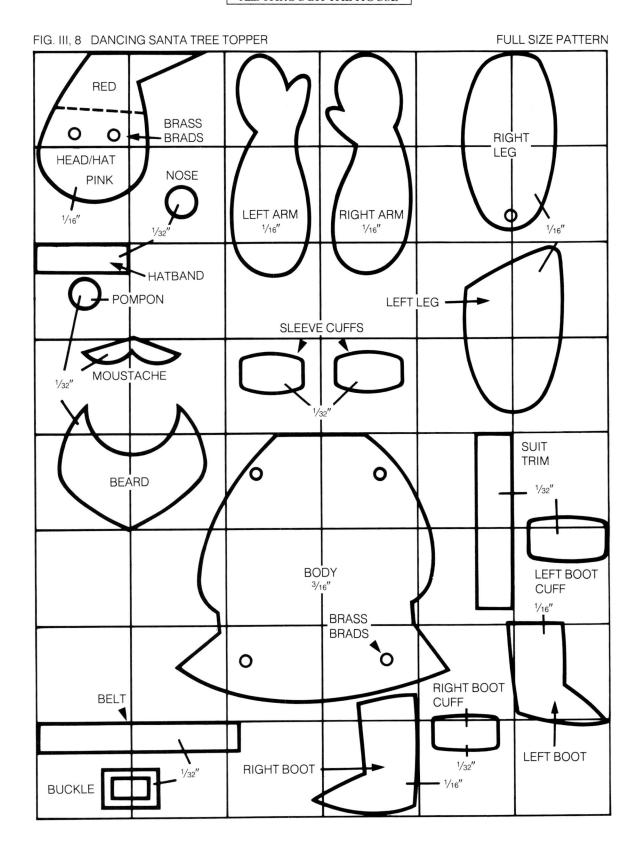

WOODEN WONDERLAND ORNAMENTS

(photos, pages 80-84)

Average: For those with some experience in woodworking.

Materials: Balsa wood planks; larger and smaller brass brads; brass wire; graphite paper; stylus or dry ballpoint pen; fine sandpaper; tack cloth; varnish; 1-inch foam brushes; craft knife; tack hammer; wire cutters; string; white glue; paper for patterns.

Directions:

1. Trace the full-size patterns in FIGS. III, 9A-9F *(pages 80-85)* onto paper. Cut out the paper patterns. Using the graphite paper and stylus or dry ballpoint pen, trace each pattern piece separately onto the balsa wood.

2. Cut out the wood pieces with the craft knife. Sand the wood pieces smooth, removing any graphite marks. Wipe off all the sawdust with the tack cloth.

3. Using the patterns and photos as placement guides, glue the wood pieces together, bottom layers first. Nail the smaller brass brads where indicated by dots on the patterns. Nail larger brass brads where indicated by circles on the patterns. For each ornament, glue a piece of balsa to the top back of the ornament, and push one end of a 2-inch length of brass wire into the balsa piece. Bend the other wire end into a hanger loop.

4. Using the foam brushes, varnish the ornaments; let dry completely.

5. Fold three 5-inch lengths of string in half, and glue them to the horse for a tail. Repeat with three 2-inch lengths of string for the horse's forelock. Wrap and glue a length of string around the bugle handle; fray the back end of the string, and let it hang below the bugle *(see photo, page 84)*.

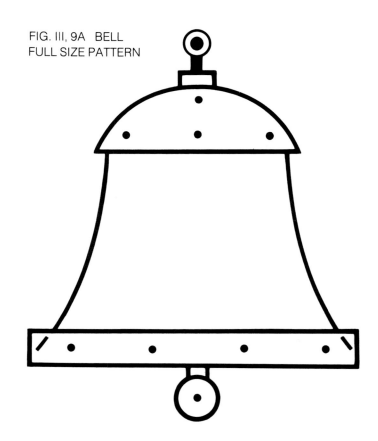

FIG. III, 9A   BELL
FULL SIZE PATTERN

FIG. III, 9B   HORSE
FULL SIZE PATTERN

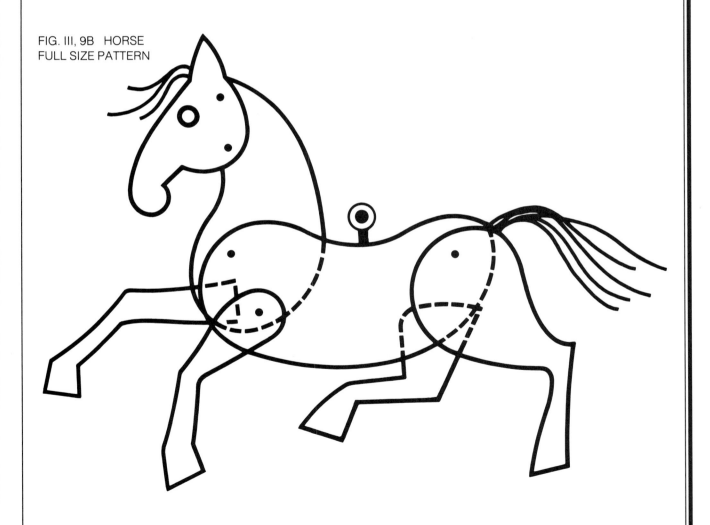

FIG. III, 9C   DOVE OF PEACE
FULL SIZE PATTERN

FIG. III, 9D   LITTLE BROWN CHURCH

FULL SIZE PATTERN

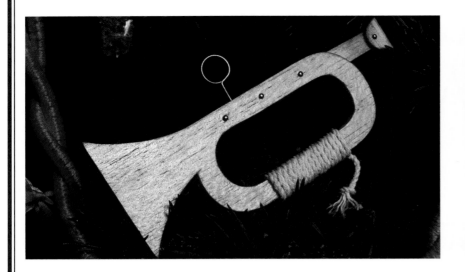

TIPS FOR A "GREEN" CHRISTMAS

A Christmas Tree with Roots!

This year, choose a Christmas tree that keeps on giving—and living! Small evergreens come in pots; larger trees have rootballs wrapped in burlap; both are available at nurseries or garden centers. After the holidays, plant the tree in your yard.

Before the ground freezes, dig a hole that is 2 feet across and at least 1½ feet deep. Cover the hole with insulating material, such as straw or leaves.

Place the soil dug out of the hole in a plastic bucket or trash can, and store it in the basement or garage to keep the soil from freezing.

Choose a tree that is no more than 4 feet tall and has fresh, not brittle, needles with signs of new growth. Have a pot or sturdy box at home in which to put the tree.

Water the tree well while it is in the house; keep the rootball moist. Set the tree in the coolest part of the room, away from heating vents, radiators or the fireplace.

Keep a live tree indoors for no more than 10 days; 4 to 5 days is best. Before planting, place the tree in a garage or basement for a few days to accustom it to the cold.

Before planting the tree, adjust the hole to be twice the size of the rootball and slightly deeper. If the tree is potted, remove it from its pot and place it in the hole. If the tree's rootball is wrapped in burlap, loosen the ties, and plant the tree as is; the burlap will disintegrate over time.

Hold the tree straight while the hole is filled in, packing soil around the rootball; the rootball top should be left slightly exposed. Then cover the planted area with a 3-inch-thick layer of mulch.

If the tree cannot be planted because the ground is frozen, keep the tree outdoors near the house or other trees. Cover its rootball or container with a 6- to 12-inch-thick layer of mulch. Plant the tree as soon as the ground thaws.

FIG. III, 9E   TOY SOLDIER

FULL SIZE PATTERN

FIG. III, 9F   BUGLE

FULL SIZE PATTERN

HERALD ANGEL TREE TOPPER

Hark! This herald angel sounds his trumpet gloriously from the top of your Christmas tree.

Average: For those with some experience in woodworking.

Materials: Balsa wood: ¼ x 4 x 8 inches, and ³⁄₃₂ x 4 x 36 inches; brass brads; spool wire; graphite paper; stylus or dry ballpoint pen; varnish; 1-inch foam brush; craft knife; tack hammer; wire cutters; white glue; sharpened pencil; paper for pattern.

Directions:

1. Enlarge the pattern in FIG. III, 10A onto paper, following the directions on page 271. Using the graphite paper and stylus or dry ballpoint pen, transfer the pattern pieces to the balsa wood; transfer the A body piece to the ¼-inch-thick balsa, and the other pattern pieces to the ³⁄₃₂-inch-thick balsa. Cut out the wood pieces with the craft knife. Also cut a ½ x 1-inch block from the ¼-inch-thick balsa.

2. Following the assembly diagrams in FIGS. III, 10B and 10C, glue the B hair, C cheek, D eye, and E left arm to the front of the A body. Glue the G leg and F right arm to the back of the A body. Glue the H horn to the mouth between the E and F arms.

3. Glue the J, K, L, M and N feathers to the I wing. Glue the O feather to the I wing on top of the J/K/L/M/N feathers. Glue the Q feather to the P wing. Glue P/Q to the I/O assembly. Let the glue dry completely. Glue the wing assembly to the A body.

4. Cut the brass brads to ¼-inch lengths. Using the pencil, make starter holes for the brads where indicated by the black dots in FIG. III, 10B. Nail the brads to the angel. Notch the balsa block to hold a piece of wire *(see* FIG. III, 10C)*, and glue the block to the back of the angel.

5. Varnish the angel, and let the varnish dry completely. Run a 6-inch length of wire through the notch in the back block. Attach the angel to the top of the tree with the wire.

FIG. III, 10A   HERALD ANGEL PATTERN   1 SQ. = 1"

FIG. III, 10B   FRONT VIEW ASSEMBLY DIAGRAM

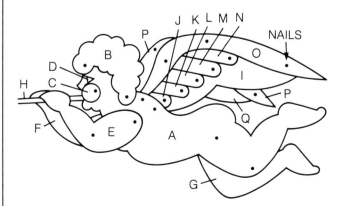

FIG. III, 10C   BACK VIEW ASSEMBLY DIAGRAM

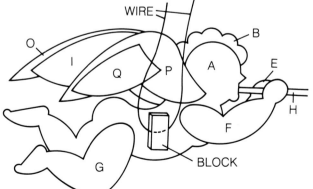

OVERNIGHT SENSATIONS

The
holly's up,
the house is all bright,
The tree is ready,
The candle alight;
Rejoice and be glad,
all children tonight!
—Carl August Peter Cornelius

What do you do when
you need a gift at the last minute? Or your holiday feast
is planned and prepared, but the house still doesn't have
that beautiful Yuletide glow?
In this chapter, we've collected our quickest and easiest
trims and gifts to help you through the hectic holidays.
Many of our table or mantel arrangements can be made
by simply grouping together a few easy-to-find items. Just
add a dab of glue, a sprinkle of glitter or a twist of wire
and you have instant Christmas cheer!
Simple gifts can be the nicest, especially when they're
hand-crafted with love by you. These timely presents will
easily fill those last-minute holes in your gift list.
Every holiday season has its crazy moments, but these
bright ideas and pretty projects can help…even if you
wait until Christmas Eve to use them!

TERRIFIC TRIMS

Lovely, down-to-the-wire decorating
projects to add Christmas cheer to any room
in the house.

A COOKIE CUTTER CHRISTMAS

Use these jolly decorations as festive accents all through your home, or to add a special touch to gifts for your friends and family.

Easy: Achievable by anyone.

COOKIE CUTTER TIES

Materials for One Tie: Holiday print fabric; 18 inches of metallic gold or silver ribbon, or satin ribbon to match or complement fabric; cookie cutter in shape desired; fusible interfacing; iron; glue *(optional)*; three small red pompons *(optional)*.

Directions:

1. Place a piece of fabric right side down with two layers of fusible interfacing over it. Place a second piece of fabric, right side up, on top of the interfacing. Fuse the layers following the fusible interfacing package directions.

2. Place the cookie cutter on the fused fabric, and trace carefully around the outer edge of the cookie cutter. Cut out the fabric shape. Repeat to make a second fabric shape.

3. At the center top of one fabric shape, pull the interfacing layers apart about ½ inch. Insert one end of the ribbon between the layers, press the layers together, and iron to fuse them again. Repeat with the second fabric shape on the opposite end of the ribbon. If you are using a holly leaf or gingerbread man cookie cutter, glue the pompons to the leaves for berries *(see photo, at left)* or to the gingerbread man for buttons.

4. Fasten the tie to a gift package, or around the neck of a jar *(see photo, above right)*. Or make a holiday wreath by fastening several ties to a grapevine or straw wreath, and adding a bow of coordinating print ribbons *(see photo, at left)*.

COOKIE CUTTER APPLIQUÉS

Materials: Holiday print fabrics; cookie cutters in shapes desired.

For Fabric Appliqués: Matching threads; fusible interfacing; iron; sewing machine. **For Wood Appliqués:** Glue; clear acrylic spray varnish.

Directions:

1. Fabric Appliqué: Place a piece of fabric right side up. Place a cookie cutter on the fabric, and trace lightly around the outer edge of the cookie cutter. Place the fabric with the tracing on top of a piece of fusible interfacing, and cut out the cookie cutter shape through both layers.

2. Place the fabric shape on the fabric object to be decorated, with the interfacing in between. Fuse the layers together following the fusible interfacing package directions.

3. Satin stitch by machine around the edges of the fabric shape.

4. Wood Appliqué: Make a fabric shape following the directions in Step 1, omitting the fusible webbing.

5. Apply a thin layer of glue evenly to the wrong side of the cookie cutter fabric shape. Place the shape carefully on the wooden object to be decorated *(see photo, above)*, and press the fabric shape lightly but firmly to make sure it adheres properly. Let the glue dry completely.

6. Spray several light coats of acrylic over both the fabric shape and the surrounding wood, letting the acrylic dry between coats.

SWEET 'N SIMPLE

Easy: Achievable by anyone.

Materials: Ceramic pot; contrasting color saucer; candy canes; sprigs of fresh juniper.

Directions:
Turn the saucer upside down, and set the ceramic pot on top of it. Hang the candy canes around the edge of the pot. Arrange the juniper sprigs around the pot, placing them in the same direction.

HOLIDAY POMANDERS

To make the fragrant centerpiece below, pile clove-studded pomanders and pine cones in a wooden bucket. Tuck in pine sprays, cinnamon sticks and a quaint ornament.

Easy: Achievable by anyone.

Materials for Five Pomanders:
5 medium-size sturdy fruits, such as apples or citrus fruits; box of whole cloves *(see Note, below)*; awl; tack hammer; pencil; ground cinnamon; orris root powder; paper bag; ribbon for hanging pomanders; straight pins for hanging pomanders.

Note: *The clove designs on the fruits in the photo let a good amount of rind show through. If you wish to cover five fruits completely, you may need more than one box of cloves.*

Directions:
1. Clove-Studded Pomanders:
Using the pencil, outline a design on each fruit rind. Make starter holes with the awl along the designs on thick-skinned fruits. Hammer the cloves in place gently. These pomanders can be used immediately.

2. Cinnamon-Coated Pomanders: Place equal amounts of ground cinnamon and orris root powder in the paper bag. Place a clove-studded pomander in the bag, and shake to coat the pomander. Repeat to coat the remaining pomanders. Place the coated pomanders in a loosely covered container for 3 to 4 weeks to allow them to dry.

3. Hanging Pomanders: Plan the clove designs on the pomanders to leave room for ribbon hangers. For each pomander, cut a length of ribbon to go completely around it once. Cut a second length of ribbon 6 inches longer than the first. Wrap the shorter length around the pomander, and pin it in place at the top and bottom. Wrap the longer length around the pomander at right angles to the first, and pin it to the bottom of the pomander. Knot the longer ribbon at the top of the pomander, and pin the knot in place. Knot the ends of the ribbon to make a loop for a hanger. Cut a third length of ribbon, tie it in a bow and pin the bow to the pomander over the knot.

HOLIDAY HAND TOWEL

For an extra-special holiday touch in the bathroom, wrap guest soaps in colored cellophane, and display them in a bowl or basket.

Easy: Achievable by anyone.

Materials: Hand towel in solid holiday color; colorfast holiday print or color ribbon with same fabric content as towel; matching thread.

Directions:
Cut a length of ribbon ½ inch longer than the width of the towel. Pin the ribbon to the towel over the towel's woven band, turning under the ribbon's raw edges ¼ inch. Edgestitch the ribbon in place, making sure the folded ribbon ends are flush with the towel's long edges.

TIPS FOR A "GREEN" CHRISTMAS

Merry Mugs

Using a mug for hot beverages in the office instead of a disposable cup cuts down tremendously on the use of paper and plastic foam. A ceramic mug makes a great gift for a co-worker. And a spill-proof mug is perfect for your favorite commuter!

Mugs come in every color imaginable, with decorations to suit every taste. Look for them in card stores, gift shops, gourmet and housewares departments, and even the grocery store.

A SYMPHONY IN SILVER

Easy: Achievable by anyone.

Materials: 7-inch-diameter twig basket with handle; 6- to 12-inch-long birch twigs; sphagnum moss; artificial mistletoe with berries; 1 yard of ¾-inch-wide silver ribbon; 1-inch-diameter silver balls with attached wires; white glitter; silver glitter; gloss Mod Podge®; 1½-inch foam brush; floral foam; floral pick; floral wire; wax paper.

Directions:

1. Cut the floral foam to fit inside the basket just below the rim. Set the foam aside.

2. Cover your work surface with wax paper. Using the foam brush, coat areas of the basket with Mod Podge. Sprinkle the wet areas with the white glitter. To achieve a more natural look, leave some basket areas unfrosted. Repeat on the basket handle, and on the birch twigs. Coat areas of the mistletoe with Mod Podge, and dust them lightly with the silver glitter.

3. Make a silver ribbon bow with streamers. Wire the floral pick to the back of the bow.

4. Place the foam in the basket, and cover the foam with the moss. Using the photo as a guide, insert the birch twigs, mistletoe, silver balls, and silver ribbon bow into the foam in a pleasing arrangement.

BY CANDLELIGHT

Easy: Achievable by anyone.

Materials: Brass candleholder; large glass hurricane shade; tall white candle; spruce branches; pine cones in assorted sizes.

Directions:

1. Set the candle in the candleholder in the center of the table. Place the glass hurricane shade over the candle and candleholder.

2. Arrange the spruce branches around the glass hurricane shade; if necessary, trim the branches to create a full-looking arrangement.

3. Set the pine cones on top of the branches in a pleasing arrangement.

RUSTIC BIRCH CANDLEHOLDERS

Tuck pine sprays around the birch candleholders for a simple and lovely centerpiece. These country-style candleholders make great gifts.

Easy: Achievable by anyone.

Materials: 2½-inch-diameter white birch logs in various lengths; tall red candles in various widths and heights; saw; drill with assorted bits.

Directions:

1. Long Candleholder: Select the longest log, and leave bits of branches on it to keep it from rolling. Steady the log on a flat surface. Drill ⅝-inch-deep holes 2 inches apart across the log. Insert different-height candles in the holes *(see photo)*.

2. Tall Candleholders: If necessary, make a straight cut on one end of each log so the log stands straight. Center and drill a ⅝-inch-deep hole in the opposite end of each log, and insert a candle. Vary the widths of the holes and candles for visual interest.

CLEVER CRAFTING

Candle Light Care

The birch candleholders shown in the photo above have a lovely rustic quality, but be careful when using them. Never leave candles burning unattended, and never let candles burn down to the ends. If you wish, place a glass bobèche, or drip catcher, at the base of each candle.

EASY MINI-WREATHS

Easy: Achievable by anyone.

Materials: Six 4-inch-diameter twig wreaths; miniature pine cones; dried rosebuds; bunches of artificial small berries with leaves; 3 miniature snow-covered evergreen trees; 3 miniature glass ball ornaments; multi-colored miniature bead ornaments; miniature mallard duck; Spanish moss; metallic-edged dark green ribbon; metallic-edged gold ribbon; loose-weave gold ribbon; gold and red satin cording; metallic gold cording; gold braid; gold star sequins; gold spray paint; floral wire; hot glue gun.

Directions:

1. Glue the miniature evergreen trees to the bottom of a wreath's center opening. Glue the gold star sequins around the wreath. Glue a metallic gold cording bow below the trees.

2. Cut short lengths of floral wire. Attach two or three bunches of berries with leaves to each wire, and wind the wires around a wreath. Wire a dark green ribbon bow with streamers to the top of the wreath.

3. Glue the multi-colored miniature bead ornaments in a cluster to the bottom of a wreath. Cut a short length of gold braid, knot it, and glue it underneath the bead ornaments. Glue the miniature glass ball ornaments around the braid knot.

4. Glue a loose-weave gold bow to the top of a wreath. Make a "nest" from the Spanish moss, and glue it to the wreath's center opening. Glue the miniature duck on top of the nest.

5. Spray paint a wreath gold, and let the paint dry. Wind gold and red satin cording around the wreath. Tie the cording ends into a bow at the top.

6. Glue miniature pine cones around a wreath. Glue dried rosebuds between the pine cones. Wire a metallic-edged gold ribbon bow with streamers to the top of the wreath.

GIFTS
IN A FLASH

Great ways to take care of last-minute
entries on your gift list.

BREAKFAST IN BED TRAY & NAPKIN RINGS

Easy: Achievable by anyone.

Materials: Wooden tray; self-sticking paper in 2 complementary holiday patterns; graphite paper; stylus or dry ballpoint pen; scissors.

Directions:

1. Tray: Measure the tray's inside edges. Cut a piece to these measurements from the first pattern self-sticking paper. Peel off the paper's backing. Lay the paper gently in position on the tray bottom, and press the paper in place.

2. Napkin Rings: Cut four 10-inch squares from the second pattern self-sticking paper. Peel the backing from the top edge of two squares. Holding the squares up to a light and matching their top corners exactly, press the squares together, wrong sides facing. If the paper's pattern is squares or plaid, match the pattern exactly. Pull off the rest of the backing carefully, smoothing the squares together from the center out as you pull. Repeat with the remaining paper squares.

3. Using the graphite paper and stylus or dry ballpoint pen, trace the full-size pattern in FIG. IV, 1 onto each double paper square. Cut out the shapes, and slash the slots where indicated on the pattern. Slide one slot through the other on each shape to close the napkin rings.

CLEVER CRAFTING

Quick Tile Trivet

Press a self-stick felt pad onto each bottom corner of a pretty tile and you have an instant trivet. Add an adhesive hanger loop centered on a back side edge so the tile can be displayed when not in use.

FIG. IV, 1 BREAKFAST IN BED TRAY AND NAPKIN RINGS

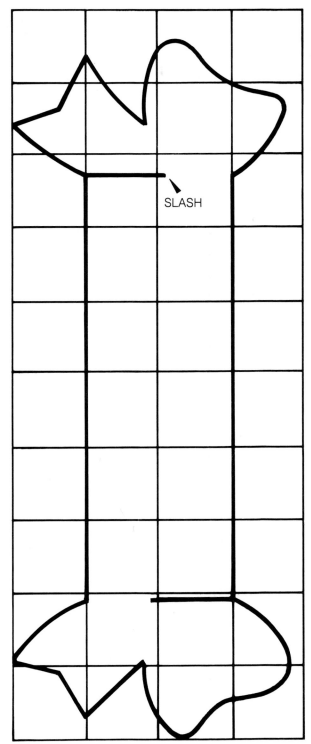

SLASH

FULL SIZE

SWEET SACHETS

*Make these sweet-smelling dainties
with inexpensive embroidered
handkerchiefs.*

Easy: Achievable by anyone.

Materials: 4 purchased
embroidered handkerchiefs, or print
fabric; matching thread; solid white
opaque fabric for backing (if using
handkerchiefs); 1¼ yards of 1-inch-
wide gathered lace; ⅔ yard of narrow
satin ribbon; 2 ounces of potpourri;
tracing paper for pattern.

Directions
(¼-inch seams allowed):
1. Heart Sachet: Trace the heart
half-pattern in FIG. IV, 2 onto folded
tracing paper. Trace the half-pattern
to the other side of the paper, and
open the paper for the full pattern.
2. If using purchased embroidered
handkerchiefs, pin a 7-inch backing
fabric square to the wrong side of
each handkerchief; treat each set as a
single piece. Cut two heart shapes
from the embroidered handkerchiefs
or print fabric. With right sides
together and edges even, machine-
baste the lace to one fabric heart,
overlapping the short ends of the lace

at the top indentation. Stitch the fabric
hearts right sides together, leaving an
opening for turning. Turn the heart
right side out, and fill it with
potpourri. Turn in the open edges,
and slipstitch the opening closed *(see
Stitch Guide, page 168)*. Cut a 12-inch
length of ribbon, and make a bow.
Sew the bow to the sachet at the top
indentation *(see photo)*.
3. Square Sachet: Make the square
sachet following the directions in
Step 2, using two 5½-inch squares cut
from the embroidered handkerchiefs
or print fabric. Attach the bow to one
corner of the sachet.

FIG. IV, 2 SWEET SACHETS   FULL SIZE

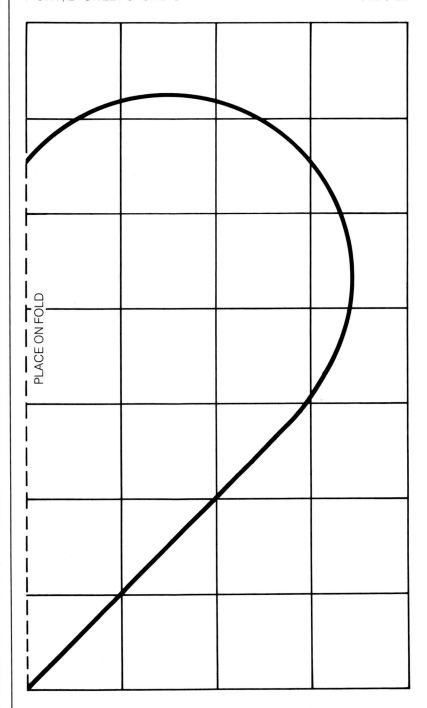

PLACE ON FOLD

TIPS FOR A "GREEN" CHRISTMAS

Potpourri Power

Stop using aerosol room fresheners! Potpourri is an all-natural, very personal way to fill your home with a lovely, subtle scent. These aromatic mixtures of herbs, flowers, fruits and spices are easy to make, and are widely available in card and gift stores, and even in some supermarkets!

Fill pretty bowls or baskets with your favorite potpourri mixture, and place the containers in every room of your house. When the scent begins to fade, just add a drop or two of essential oil (available at craft shops and some natural food stores) to the potpourri to refresh it. For extra scent, place a drop of essential oil on a light bulb; as the bulb warms the oil, it becomes more fragrant.

TAKE A NOTE! BOOK

Easy: Achievable by anyone.

Materials: Two 3¼ x 5½-inch, and one ⅝ x 5½-inch mat boards; 5¼ x 6½ inches, and 1½ x 5 inches of book cloth; 3¼ x 6½ inches of decorative paper for front cover; sturdy paper for pockets; two 3 x 5-inch note pads; white glue; scissors.

Directions:

1. Lap the decorative paper ¼ inch over the larger book cloth rectangle along a 6½-inch edge. Glue the paper in place; let the glue dry completely.

2. Spread glue over the wrong side of the decorative paper and book cloth. Place the mat boards on the wrong side of the paper and cloth, with the narrow board strip centered for a spine between the wider board covers. Leave ⅛ inch between the strip and each cover, and a ½-inch border around the outside edges. Turn the border up and over the edges of the boards. Glue the border in place, mitering the corners.

3. Center the narrow book cloth strip over the inside of the spine, and glue the cloth in place.

4. Cut two 5 x 6-inch rectangles from the pocket paper. Fold each rectangle to make a flat tube, butting the rectangle's short ends at the center back. Spread glue on the backs of the paper tubes, and attach a tube to the inside of each cover for a pocket. Let the glue dry completely.

5. Slip the note pads into the pockets.

TIPS FOR A "GREEN" CHRISTMAS

Gifts From the Farm

A gift of local fruit, nuts or cheese, or a bottle of domestic wine is always welcome, and your purchases help support American farmers. Search the aisles of a supermarket for some great last-minute gifts.

● Red and green apples in a basket for your child's teacher.

● A decorative jar filled with red and white pistachios for your secretary.

● A chunk of Wisconsin or Vermont Cheddar cheese, or California Monterey Jack cheese for a neighbor.

● Your favorite wine from a local winery for a family member who lives out of town.

● A mixture of nuts, chopped dates and raisins you made yourself for a holiday hostess.

THE DESK SET

Easy: Achievable by anyone.

Materials: Beige imitation leather pencil holder, letter holder and ledger desk set; rust and dark blue acrylic paints; 2 natural sponges; old newspapers.

Directions:

1. Dip a sponge in the rust-colored paint. Dab the sponge on a sheet of newspaper to remove excess paint, and to check the effect created. Adjust the amount of paint on the sponge until you are satisfied with the effect. Dab the rust-colored paint on the imitation leather surfaces of the desk set, letting the beige color show through underneath. Let the paint dry completely.

2. Repeat with the dark blue paint and remaining sponge until you have achieved the desired effect. Let the paint dry completely.

"DESIGNER" BATH TOWELS

Easy: Achievable by anyone.

Materials: Set of solid color bath towels; contrasting print fabric from bed sheets or fabric scraps; matching thread; sewing machine.

Directions:

Cut a print fabric strip ½ inch longer than the width of one of the towels. Pin the strip to the towel along the towel's bottom edge, or 3 inches above the bottom edge, turning under the long raw edges ¼ inch as you pin. Turn under the strip's short ends ¼ inch. Edgestitch around all the strip edges. Repeat on the remaining towels.

PRESENTS
PRESENTS
PRESENTS!

"I
want some crackers,
And I want some candy;
I think a box of chocolates
Would come in handy;
I don't mind oranges,
I do like nuts!
And I should like a pocket-knife
That really cuts.
And, oh! Father Christmas, if you love me at all,
Bring me a big, red india-rubber ball!"
—A. A. Milne

Since that miraculous
night when the Magi knelt to offer gold, frankincense and
myrrh to the babe in the manger, Christmas has been
celebrated by giving to those we love.

A gift created by hand is especially cherished. The time
and effort spent to knit a sweater, craft a wooden toy, or
stitch a pretty doll shows that special someone how
much you care.

In this chapter you'll find presents for the home, for her,
for him, and for the little ones in your life. Choose from
projects such as a snuggly afghan, woolly sweaters,
wonderful wooden toys, a marquetry box, a trio of pastel
dollies, winter-warm mittens, and so much more. There's
sure to be something here for everyone on your list!

Some of these crafts take time to finish. You'll probably
want to start them early, so they'll be done before the
holiday rush. Others can be done at the last minute, and
tucked under the tree on Christmas Eve.

Giving a handmade gift is like giving a part of yourself—
and there's no better way to make this Christmas special.

GIFTS
FOR THE HOME

From your heart and hands
to a special someone's home—what better
way to say "I love you" at Christmas time?

PINEAPPLE AFGHAN

(60 x 56 inches)
The eternal symbol of hospitality decorates this extra-warm afghan.

Average: For those with some experience in knitting, crocheting and embroidery.

Materials: Reynolds Bulky Reynelle yarn (2-ounce skein): 29 skeins of Natural (A); Reynolds Reynelle yarn (4-ounce skein): 2 skeins each of Navy (B) and Light Gold (C), and 1 skein each of Cardinal (D), Loden (E) and Clay (F); 1 pair size 10 knitting needles, OR ANY SIZE NEEDLES TO OBTAIN GAUGE BELOW; size I crochet hook; No. 16 tapestry needle.

Gauge: In Stockinette Stitch (st st), 3 sts = 1 inch; 9 rows = 2 inches.

Note: *Use a single strand of Bulky Reynelle yarn, and a double strand of Reynelle yarn throughout.*

Directions:

1. Pineapple Panel (make 3): With the knitting needles and A, cast on 23 sts. Work in st st (k 1 row, p 1 row) for 240 rows. Bind off.

2. Long Side Edging, Row 1: With the right side facing and the crochet hook, join A in the right-hand corner of a long edge, and ch 1. Working into the sides of the knit rows and keeping the edge flat, sc in each of first 2 rows, * [sk 1 row, sc in next row] twice; sk 1 row, sc in next 2 rows; rep from * to the end of the long edge. **Row 2:** Ch 1, turn, sc in each sc across. Fasten off. Rep Rows 1 and 2 of the Long Side Edging along the opposite edge.

3. Embroidery: With yarn, mark off 4 sets of 60 rows on each Pineapple Panel for the beginning and end of the pineapple design. Using a double strand of yarn in the tapestry needle, and beginning at the lower edge of each Panel, work the pineapple design in FIG. V, 1A in duplicate stitch on each Pineapple Panel *(see Stitch Guide, page 168).*

4. Motif Panel (make 4): With the knitting needles and A, cast on 19 sts. Work in st st for 240 rows. Bind off. Work the Long Side Edgings on each Motif Panel following Step 2. Using a double strand of yarn in the tapestry needle, beginning at the lower edge of each Panel, and repeating Rows 1 to 11 to the upper edge, work the alternate design in FIG. V, 1B in duplicate stitch on each Motif Panel.

5. Blocking: Place each Panel wrong side up on a towel, pin to size, and cover with a damp towel. Run a warm, dry iron lightly over the towel; *do not press.* Let the Panels dry completely.

6. Joining: With the crochet hook or tapestry needle and A, alternating Pineapple Panels with Motif Panels, and working through both lps of the sc edges, sew or sl st the Panels tog, beginning and ending with a Motif Panel. From the right side with A, work 1 row sl st along each side edge of the afghan. Block the edges flat.

7. Top Edging, Row 1: With the right side facing and the crochet hook, join A in the upper right-hand corner, and ch 1. Keeping the edge flat, sc along the top edge, working a multiple of 9 sts plus 6. **Rows 2 and 3:** Ch 1, turn, sc in each sc across. Fasten off. Turn. **Row 4 (wrong side):** Join 2 strands of D in the first sc, ch 1, sc in same sc, ch 7, sk 4 sc, sc in next sc, * ch 3, sk 3 sc, sc in next sc, ch 7, sk 4 sc, sc in next sc; rep from * across. **Row 5:** Ch 1, turn, 9 sc in first ch-7 sp, * ch 3, sk ch-3 sp, 9 sc in next ch-7 sp; rep from * across. Fasten off. Turn. **Row 6:** Join A in first sc, ch 1, sc in same sc, ch 8, sk 7 sc, sc in last sc of same group, * ch 3, sc in first sc of next 9-sc group, ch 8, sc in last sc of same group; rep from * across. Turn. **Row 7:** Sl st in first ch-8 lp; ch 3, 9 dc in same lp, * sk ch-3, 10 dc in next ch-8 lp; rep from * across. Fasten off. Work the Top Edging along the bottom edge. Pin the afghan to the finished measurements, and block it following Step 5.

FIG. V, 1A PINEAPPLE DESIGN

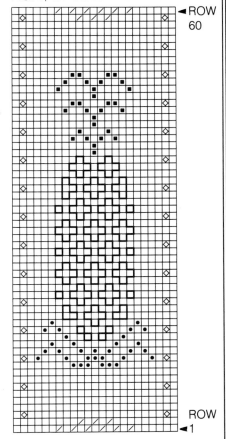

ROW 60

ROW 1

FIG. V, 1B ALTERNATE DESIGN

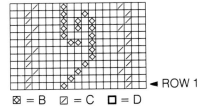

ROW 1

⊠ = B   ⊡ = C   ☐ = D
▪ = E   ● = F

PENNSYLVANIA DUTCH FOOTSTOOL

Average: For those with some experience in decorative painting.

Materials: Purchased wooden footstool (available at craft supply stores); graphite paper; stylus or dry ballpoint pen; medium-fine sandpaper; tack cloth; white acrylic paint; cadmium red light, burnt alizarin, leaf green light, leaf green medium, leaf green dark, burnt umber, and black oil paints; clear oil-based antiquing glaze; wood sealer; clear acrylic spray varnish; oil-based varnish; odorless turpentine; artist's paintbrushes: No. 6 or 8 small PH Red Sable, No. 10 or 12 medium-size PH Red Sable, No. 14 or 16 large PH Red Sable, and No. 1 liner or scroll brush; sponge brushes; palette; palette knife; wide mouth container for turpentine; soft rags; masking tape; tracing paper for patterns.

Directions:

1. Mix burnt umber paint with turpentine to make a stain. Spread the stain on the footstool with a clean rag. Wipe off the stain with another clean rag, wiping off more stain in the design area on each long stool side *(see photo).* If you wish, repeat to make the stain darker. Let the stain dry completely. Apply a coat of wood sealer, and let it dry. Sand the footstool lightly, and wipe off all the sawdust with the tack cloth.

2. Using a sponge brush and white acrylic paint, and the photo as a placement guide, paint the oval design area on the stool top. Let the paint dry. Seal the design area by spraying with several light coats of clear acrylic varnish.

3. Trace the full-size half pattern for the stool side design in Fig. V, 2A onto folded tracing paper. Trace the design onto the other half of the paper, and open the paper for the full design.

Trace the full-size quarter pattern for the stool top design in Fig. V, 2B onto tracing paper folded into quarters. Trace the design onto the remaining quarters, and open the paper for the full design. Using the graphite paper and stylus or dry ballpoint pen, center and transfer the designs to the top and both long sides of the footstool.

4. Squeeze the oil paints onto the palette. Use the turpentine to thin the reds to the consistency of soft butter, and the greens to the consistency of heavy cream. Using the large paintbrush, paint the tulips cadmium red light. If you wish, wipe the brush and apply a little burnt alizarin to the left side of each tulip, blending the colors together where they meet.

5. Paint the comma strokes above the stool top tulips cadmium red light; mix in some burnt alizarin for the larger strokes. Paint the large green comma strokes with thinned leaf green dark, the medium-size strokes

with leaf green medium, and the small strokes with leaf green light. Using the liner or scroll brush, outline the edge of the white oval design area with black *(see photo).*

6. Let the paint dry completely; this will take several days depending on the temperature, humidity and air circulation. When the paint is completely dry, apply a coat of oil-based varnish to the entire footstool.

7. Mix a little burnt umber paint into a tablespoon of the antiquing glaze. Brush the antiquing mixture over the entire footstool. Use a clean rag to wipe off as much of the antiquing glaze as you wish. Let the glaze dry completely, and apply a final coat of oil-based varnish.

FIG. V, 2A PENNSYLVANIA DUTCH FOOTSTOOL SIDE

FULL SIZE

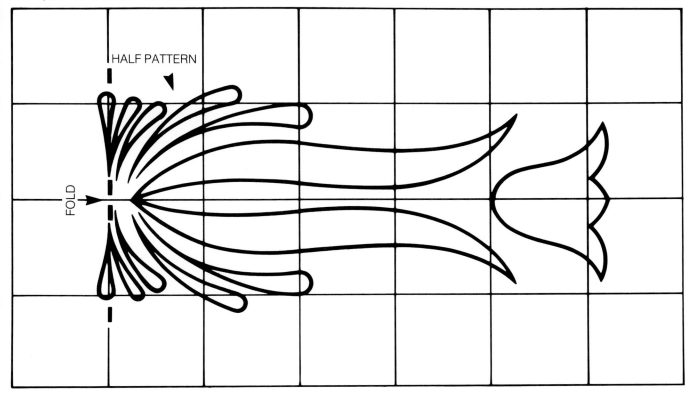

FIG. V, 2B STOOL TOP

FULL SIZE

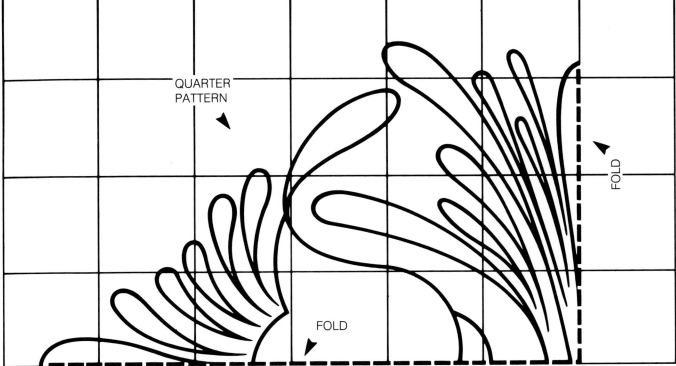

PUPPY PALACE

Average: For those with some experience in woodworking.

Materials: 4 x 8-foot panel of ⅜-inch APA 303 roughsawn plywood siding; galvanized nails; wood glue; graphite paper; stylus or dry ballpoint pen; sandpaper; tack cloth; exterior paint in color desired; paintbrush; table saw, band saw, or circular saw; sabre saw; hammer; paper for patterns.

Directions:

1. Draw the house pieces on the plywood panel following the measurements in FIG. V, 3A. If you are using a table or band saw, draw the house pieces on the face of the panel. If you are using a circular or sabre saw, draw the house pieces on the back of the panel. Leave space between the house pieces for kerf. Cut out the house pieces.

2. For the ramp and front opening, enlarge the patterns in FIGS. V, 3B and 3C *(page 112)* onto paper, following the directions on page 169. Using the graphite paper and stylus or dry ballpoint pen, transfer the ramp pattern to the back of the plywood panel. Transfer the front opening pattern to the back of the front piece. Use the sabre saw with a fine blade to make the ragged cuts on the ramp and front opening. Set aside the front opening cutout.

3. Nail the floor support cleats to the sides, front and back. Nail the front and back to the sides. Drop in the floor, and glue and nail it to the floor support cleats.

4. Nail two 12-inch roof pieces to the front and back as the lower roof pieces. Overlap the remaining roof pieces 1 inch over the lower roof pieces, and glue and nail the upper pieces in place, butting them together at the roof peak. Fit trim pieces around the outside corners of the

house, and nail the trims in place *(see* FIG. V, 3D, *page 113)*.

5. If you are making a chimney, glue and nail the chimney pieces to form an open box. Glue and nail trims around the chimney top. Glue and nail the chimney to the roof *(see* FIG. V, 3D, *and photo)*.

6. Place the ramp in the front opening, and nail the ramp to the floor. Glue and nail the front opening cutout to the outside back.

7. Sand the rough edges of the house smooth, and wipe off all the sawdust with the tack cloth. Paint the house.

FIG. V, 3A   PUPPY PALACE HOUSE PIECES

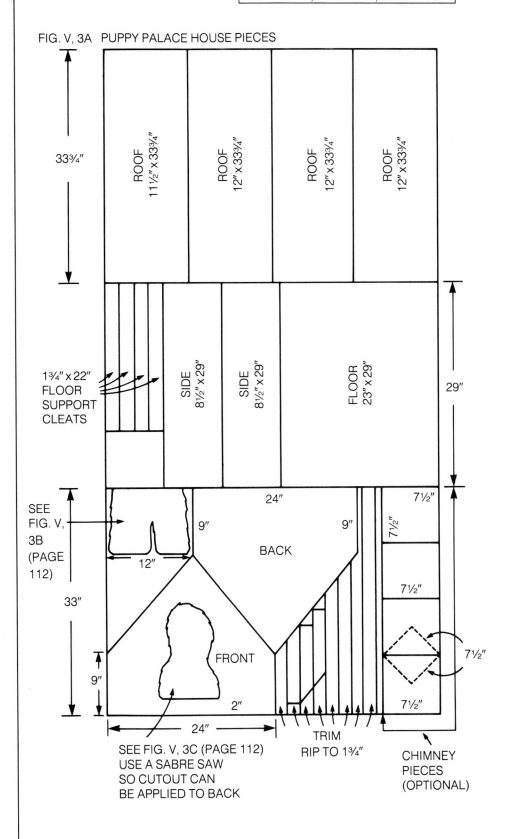

33¾"

ROOF
11½" x 33¾"

ROOF
12" x 33¾"

ROOF
12" x 33¾"

ROOF
12" x 33¾"

1¾" x 22"
FLOOR
SUPPORT
CLEATS

SIDE
8½" x 29"

SIDE
8½" x 29"

FLOOR
23" x 29"

29"

SEE
FIG. V,
3B
(PAGE
112)

9"

12"

24"

BACK

9"

7½"

7½"

7½"

33"

9"

FRONT

2"

7½"

7½"

24"

SEE FIG. V, 3C (PAGE 112)
USE A SABRE SAW
SO CUTOUT CAN
BE APPLIED TO BACK

TRIM
RIP TO 1¾"

CHIMNEY
PIECES
(OPTIONAL)

FIG. V, 3B RAMP   1 SQ. = 1″

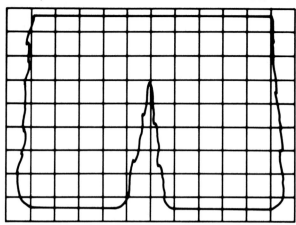

FIG. V, 3C FRONT OPENING   1 SQ. = 1″

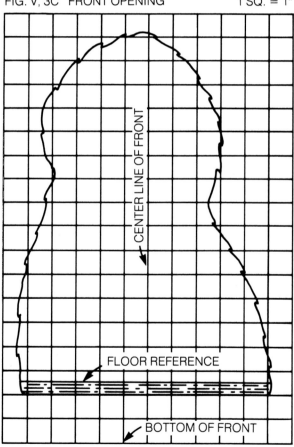

CENTER LINE OF FRONT

FLOOR REFERENCE

BOTTOM OF FRONT

FIG. V, 3D ASSEMBLY DIAGRAM

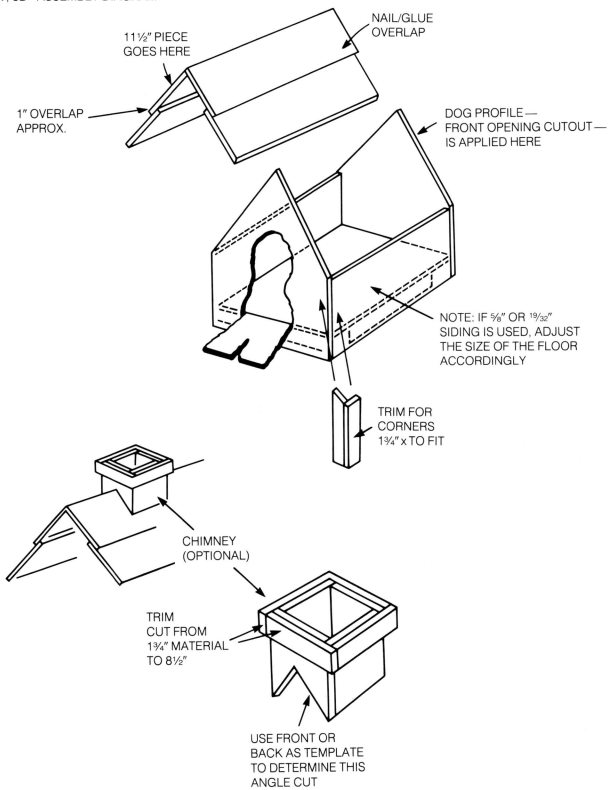

11½" PIECE
GOES HERE

NAIL/GLUE
OVERLAP

1" OVERLAP
APPROX.

DOG PROFILE—
FRONT OPENING CUTOUT—
IS APPLIED HERE

NOTE: IF ⅝" OR ¹⁹⁄₃₂"
SIDING IS USED, ADJUST
THE SIZE OF THE FLOOR
ACCORDINGLY

TRIM FOR
CORNERS
1¾" x TO FIT

CHIMNEY
(OPTIONAL)

TRIM
CUT FROM
1¾" MATERIAL
TO 8½"

USE FRONT OR
BACK AS TEMPLATE
TO DETERMINE THIS
ANGLE CUT

ESPECIALLY
FOR HER

Pretty and practical presents for mothers,
daughters, sisters and best friends.

WOMAN'S ARAN KNIT SWEATER

Challenging: Requires more experience in knitting.

Directions are given for Size Petite (6). Changes for Sizes Small (8-10), Medium (12-14) and Large (16) are in parentheses.

Materials: Bernat Blarney Spun 100% wool (50-gram ball): 17 (18, 19, 20) balls of Natural; 1 pair each size 5 and size 8 knitting needles, OR ANY SIZE NEEDLES TO OBTAIN GAUGE BELOW; 1 double-pointed needle (dp); 4 stitch holders; stitch marker; tapestry needle.

Gauge: With size 8 needles in Stockinette Stitch (st st; k 1 row, p 1 row), 9 sts = 2 inches; 6 rows = 1 inch. In Aran Patterns over center sts, 68 sts = 12 inches.

Note: *The sweater is loose fitting.*

Aran Pattern I (worked over even number of sts), Rows 1 and 2: K across. ***Rows 3 and 4:*** * K 1, p 1; rep from * across. Rep Rows 1 to 4 for Pat I.

Aran Pattern II (worked over 5 sts), Row 1: * Through back lp knit 2nd st on needle, leave on needle, k first st, sl both sts off needle *, p 1; rep between * once. ***Row 2:*** *Sk 1 st, p 2nd st on left-hand needle, leave original st on needle, p skipped st, take 2 original sts off left-hand needle—**PT made;** k 1, PT.* Rep Rows 1 and 2 for Pat II.

Aran Pattern III (worked over 11 sts), Row 1: P 2, k 7, p 2. ***Rows 2 and 4:*** K 2, p 7, k 2. ***Row 3:*** P 2, sl next 2 sts to dp needle, hold in back of work, k 1, k 2 off dp needle, k 1, sl next st to dp needle, hold in front of work, k 2, k 1 off dp needle, p 2. Rep Rows 1 to 4 for Pat III.

Aran Pattern IV (worked over 26 sts), Row 1: P 3, *sl next st to dp*

needle, hold in back of work, k 1, k 1 off dp needle — ***C2 made;*** [p 4, C2] 3 times; p 3. ***Row 2 and All Even Numbered Rows through 12:*** K the k sts, and p the p sts. ***Row 3:*** P 2, *sl next p st to dp needle, hold in back of work, k 1, p 1 off dp needle —* ***RT made;*** *sl next k st to dp needle, hold in front of work, p 1, k 1 off dp needle—***LT made;** [p 2, RT, LT] 3 times; p 2. ***Row 5:*** P 1, [RT, p 2, LT] 4 times; p 1. ***Row 7:*** P 1, k 1, [p 4, C2] 3 times; p 4, k 1, p 1. ***Row 9:*** P 1, [LT, p 2, RT] 4 times; p 1. ***Row 11:*** P 2, [LT, RT, p 2] 4 times. Rep Rows 1 to 12 for Pat IV.

Measurements:

SIZES:	PETITE	SMALL	MEDIUM	LARGE
	(6)	(8-10)	(12-14)	(16)
BODY BUST:	30½″	32½″	36″	38″

Finished Measurements:

BUST:	35″	38″	40½″	43½″

WIDTH ACROSS BACK OR FRONT AT UNDERARMS:

	17½″	19″	20¼″	21¾″

WIDTH ACROSS SLEEVE AT UPPER ARM:

	14½″	15¼″	16¼″	17″

Directions:

1. Back: Starting at the lower edge with size 5 needles, cast on 74 (80, 86, 92) sts. Work in twist ribbing as follows: ***Row 1:*** * P 1, through back lp k next st twisting st; rep from * across. Rep Row 1 for pat to 2½ inches, inc 20 sts evenly spaced across last row — 94 (100, 106, 112) sts. Change to size 8 needles and Pats. ***Row 1 (right side):*** Following Row 1 of each Aran Pattern, work as follows: Pat I over 12 (14, 18, 20) sts; p 1 (2, 1, 2); * Pat II over 5 sts, Pat III over 11 sts, Pat II over 5 sts, * Pat IV over 26 sts; rep between * once; p 1 (2, 1, 2); Pat I over 12 (14, 18, 20) sts. ***Row 2:*** Following Row 2 of each Aran Pattern, work as follows: Pat I over 12 (14, 18, 20) sts; k 1 (2, 1, 2); * Pat II over 5 sts, Pat III over 11 sts, Pat II over 5 sts *, Pat IV over 26 sts; rep between *

once; k 1 (2, 1, 2); Pat I over 12 (14, 18, 20) sts. Keeping to the Pats as established, work to 15½ inches from beg, or desired length, ending with a wrong side row.

2. Armhole Shaping: Keeping to Pats, bind off 5 (6, 7, 8) sts at beg of next 2 rows. Dec 1 st each end every other row 5 times — 74 (78, 82, 86) sts. Work even in Pats until armholes measure 7½ (8, 8½, 9) inches, ending with a wrong side row.

3. Shoulder Shaping: Keeping to Pats, bind off 8 (8, 9, 9) sts at beg of next 4 (2, 6, 4) rows, then bind off 9 (9, 0, 10) sts at beg of next 2 (4, 0, 2) rows. Bind off remaining 24 (26, 28, 30) sts for the Back Neck edge.

4. Pocket Linings (make 2): With size 8 needles, cast on 24 sts. Beg with Row 1, work in Pat I for 12 rows. Sl these sts to a st holder.

5. Front: Work the same as the Back until 12 rows above the ribbing band.

6. Pocket Opening, Left Side: Keeping to Pats, work 15 (18, 21, 24) sts, sl remaining sts to another st holder to be worked later, sl 24 lining sts to free needle. Keeping to Pat I, work these 24 sts. These sts will be worked in Pat I until pocket opening is completed. Work 5 inches, ending with a right side row. ***Last Row:*** Bind off 24 lining sts, complete row. Leave yarn attached. Slip these sts to a st holder. Sl center 64 sts from holder to a size 8 needle. Work to the same length as the end of the Pocket Opening, ending with a wrong side row. Break off yarn. Sl these sts to a st holder. Work 24 lining sts, then the remaining 15 (18, 21, 24) sts from st holder. Work the same as the Left Side, reversing the shaping. ***Joining Row:*** Beg at the Left Side edge in Pats, work 15 (18, 21, 24) sts, 64 center sts, and 15 (18, 21, 24) Right Side sts. Work the same as the Back to 6 rows after the start of the Armhole Shaping — 80 (84, 88, 92) sts.

7. Neck Shaping, Row 1: Dec 1 st at the Armhole edge, and work until 27 (28, 29, 30) sts are on needle; join a 2nd ball of yarn, bind off center 24 (26, 28, 30) sts; work to last 2 sts, dec 1 st — 27 (28, 29, 30) sts each side of the Neck. Working both sides at once, dec 1 st at each Armhole edge every other row twice more — 25 (26, 27, 28) sts each side of the Neck. Work until Armholes measure the same as the Back to the Shoulders. Shape the Shoulders the same as on the Back.

8. Sleeves: Starting at the lower edge of the Sleeve with size 5 needles, cast on 40 (44, 48, 52) sts. Work in twist ribbing following Step 1 to 3 inches, inc 15 sts evenly spaced across last row — 55 (59, 63, 67) sts. Change to size 8 needles and Pats. **Row 1 (right side):** Following Row 1 of each Aran Pattern, work as follows: Pat I over 16 (18, 20, 22) sts; p 1; Pat II over 5 sts, Pat III over 11 sts, Pat II over 5 sts; p 1; Pat I over 16 (18, 20, 22) sts. Keeping to the Pats as established, inc 1 st each end every 12th row 6 times. Work the new sts into Pat I — 67 (71, 75, 79) sts. Work to 17 inches from the beg, or the desired length, ending with a wrong side row (same Pat row as at the underarms of the Back).

9. Cap Shaping: Keeping to Pats, bind off 5 (6, 7, 8) sts at beg of next 2 rows. Dec 1 st each end every other row 16 (17, 18, 19) times. Bind off 5 sts at beg of next 5 rows.

10. Collar: With size 8 needles, cast on 25 (26, 27, 28) sts. Work in Pat I. Work 4 rows. Inc 1 st at beg of next row, then every 4th row 8 times more — 34 (35, 36, 37) sts. Work even until the Collar is long enough to reach within ½ inch of the Back Neck edge, ending at the straight edge of the Collar. **Short Rows:** Keeping to Pat, work 28 (29, 30, 31) sts, *turn,* sl 1, work to end, *turn,* work 22 (23, 24, 25) sts, *turn,* sl 1, work to end, *turn,* work 16 (17, 18, 19) sts, *turn,* sl 1, work to end, *turn,* work 10 (11, 12, 13) sts, *turn,* sl 1, work to end. Work over all sts for 3 rows. Mark for the center back. Work 3 rows. Rep Short Rows. Continue as for the first side of the Collar, working decreases instead of increases.

11. Finishing: Sew the Shoulder, side and Sleeve seams. Sew the lower right edge of the Collar to the Front Neck edge. Sew the lower left edge of the Collar to the Front Neck edge under the right edge. Sew the Collar to the Front Neck edge. Sew in the Sleeves. Sew down the Pocket Linings. Block the sweater to the finished measurements following the directions on page 167.

SWEETHEART SWEATER

Average: For those with some experience in knitting.

Directions are given for Size Small. Changes for Sizes Medium and Large are in parentheses.

Materials: Patons Diana yarn (50-gram ball): 9 (9, 10) balls of Barley (MC), and 4 (4, 5) balls of Dusty Pink (CC); 1 pair each size 6 and size 9 knitting needles, OR ANY SIZE NEEDLES TO OBTAIN GAUGE BELOW; 2 stitch holders; stitch markers; tapestry needle.

Gauge: On size 9 needles in Stockinette Stitch (st st), 4 sts = 1 inch; 5 rows = 1 inch.

Measurements:

SIZES:	SMALL	MEDIUM	LARGE
BODY BUST:	32"-34"	36"-38"	40"-42"

Finished Measurements:

BUST:	36"	40"	44"

Directions:

1. Back: With size 6 needles and CC, cast on 73 (81, 89) sts. Work in k 1, p 1 ribbing for 2 inches. Change to size 9 needles. Join MC; do not cut CC. ***Row 1 (right side):*** Following FIG. V, 4A *(page 118)* as marked for Body, starting on Row 1 at size chosen (S, M, L), k through center st; starting at next st, read the chart back to S (M, L) to complete the row. ***Row 2:*** Reading FIG. V, 4A, Row 2 as above, p 1 row. Continue in st st (k 1 row, p 1 row) through Row 22. Work 2 rows of MC. Work Row 25 (snowflake row). Work 4 rows of MC. Work Row 30 (snowflake row). Repeat a snowflake row every 5th row, placing the snowflake sts between the snowflake sts of the row below. Work even in the established pat until 15 inches from beg, or desired length to the underarm. End on MC row.

2. Armhole: Mark each end of the last row for beg of the Armhole.

Beg Fig.V, 4B at size chosen for Body, reading it the same as Fig. V, 4A. Work Rows 1 to 26, then work Rows 25 to 1 in that order. If additional rows are needed to complete Armhole length, work MC rows and snowflake rows as for Body. When Armhole measures 10 (10½, 11) inches, end with a p row.

3. Shoulder Shaping: Bind off 23 (25, 27) sts at beg of next 2 rows. Place remaining 27 (31, 35) sts on a st holder for the Back Neck.

4. Front: Work same as the Back to 7 (7½, 8) inches above the Armhole markers, ending with a p row.

5. Neck Shaping: K 30 (34, 38) sts, sl 13 sts to another st holder for the Front Neck; attach a new ball of yarn, k 30 (34, 38) sts. Working both sides at the same time, dec 1 st at the Neck edge every row 7 (9, 11) times. Work even on 23 (25, 27) sts until the Armhole measures the same as the Back. Bind off all sts.

6. Sleeves: With size 6 needles and CC, cast on 37 (41, 43) sts. Work in k 1, p 1 ribbing for 2 inches. Inc 16 (16, 18) sts across last row—53 (57, 61) sts. Change to size 9 needles. Attach MC; do not cut CC. Following Fig. V, 4A as marked for Sleeve, starting on Row 1 at size chosen (S, M, L), work the same as the Back, and at the same time inc 1 st each side every 5th row 14 times—81 (85, 89) sts. Work even to 16 (16½, 17) inches from beg, ending on MC row. Work Rows 1 to 8 of Fig. V, 4B. Bind off all sts loosely.

7. Neckband: Sew the left Shoulder seam. With the right side facing you, size 6 needles and CC, k 27 (31, 35) sts from the Back holder, pick up 15 sts along the left Neck edge, k 13 sts from the Front holder, pick up 16 sts along the right Neck edge—71 (75, 79) sts. Work in k 1, p 1 ribbing for 1 inch. Bind off loosely in ribbing. Sew the right Shoulder seam and Neckband seam. Mark the center of the Sleeve, place it at the Shoulder seam, and sew in the Sleeve between markers. Sew side and Sleeve seams.

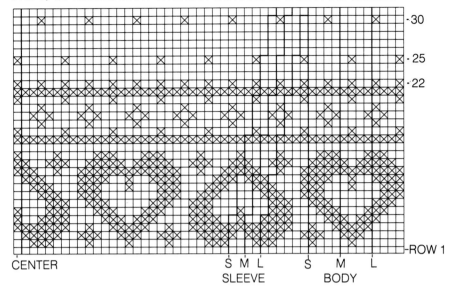

FIG. V, 4A SWEETHEART SWEATER BOTTOM OF BODY AND SLEEVE

·30

· 25

·22

ROW 1

CENTER   S M L   S   M   L
            SLEEVE   BODY

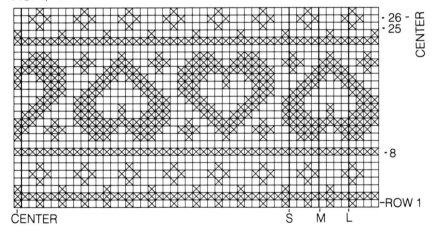

FIG. V, 4B YOKE

· 26 -
· 25

CENTER

· 8

ROW 1

CENTER   S   M   L

SEASON'S GREETINGS

118

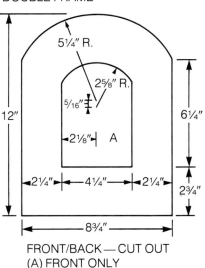

FIG. V, 5 VICTORIAN
DOUBLE FRAME

FRONT/BACK — CUT OUT
(A) FRONT ONLY

VICTORIAN DOUBLE FRAME

(holds two 5 x 7-inch photos)

Challenging: Requires more experience in crafting.

Materials: ½ yard of mauve moire taffeta; 1¼ yards of ecru cluny lace; 1¼ yards of 1½-inch-wide ecru ruffled lace; 1 yard of ¼-inch-wide mauve ribbon; ½ yard of ¼-inch-wide burgundy ribbon; lace appliqué; 3 large ribbon roses; synthetic stuffing; iron-on fusing tape; craft knife; very sharp scissors; straight pins; compass; ruler; white glue; corrugated cardboard.

Directions:

1. Using the compass and ruler, draw a frame front and frame back on the cardboard following the dimensions in FIG. V, 5. Cut out the frame front and back with the craft knife; cut out the center opening on the frame front only. Also cut two 9 x 2¼-inch cardboard spacer strips, and one 8¾ x 2¾-inch cardboard spacer strip. Cut two 9¾ x 13-inch pieces from the

taffeta. Trim the top edge of each taffeta piece to match the frame top curve plus 1 inch; do not cut out the center opening in the taffeta. Repeat for the second frame.

2. For each frame, glue the spacer strips to the inside of the frame front, placing the longer strips on the sides and the shorter strip on the bottom. Let the glue dry.

3. Place each frame front face down on the wrong side of a taffeta piece. Fold the taffeta around the straight edges of each frame front, over the spacers, and glue the taffeta in place, mitering the corners. On the curved edge, slash the taffeta every ½ inch to within ¼ inch of the cardboard. Glue the tabs in place, keeping the taffeta smooth. Repeat on the frame backs.

4. On each frame front, push small pieces of stuffing between the cardboard and taffeta through the center opening in the cardboard. Be sure the stuffing is evenly distributed and smooth; lumps will spoil the look of the taffeta. Pack the stuffing tightly to the edges of the center opening.

5. On each frame front, use the scissors to cut out a center opening

in the taffeta that is ½ to ¾ inch smaller than the cardboard opening. Slash the taffeta allowance every ½ inch all around. With the frame front facing you, pin the tabs securely to the cardboard behind the opening, pulling the taffeta taut. When the tabs are securely fastened and the taffeta lies smooth and even, turn over the frame front, and glue the tabs to the cardboard without removing the pins. Let the glue dry completely before removing the pins.

6. Glue cluny lace around each center opening *(see photo)*.

7. Cut a 4 x 9½-inch taffeta strip, and fold it in half lengthwise. Insert a same-length piece of fusing tape inside the folded strip. Press with an iron to fuse the taffeta layers together to make a frame hinge. Turn the two frame backs wrong side up, and place them side by side, ½ inch apart, with their bottom edges even. Glue the hinge lengthwise to the frame backs. Glue ruffled lace to each frame back from the bottom left corner up the side, across the top, and down the other side; do not glue lace across the bottom. Let the glue dry completely.

8. Glue each frame front to a frame back on the spacer strips, leaving the top edge open to insert a photo. Using the photo as a placement guide, trim the double frame with the lace appliqué, ribbon roses, and mauve and burgundy ribbons tied into bows with streamers.

TIPS FOR A "GREEN" CHRISTMAS

Terrific Ties!

Tie your Christmas gifts with yarn instead of ribbon. One skein of red, white or green yarn will trim many gifts at relatively little cost. Plus, your "crafty" friends will find a way to put the yarn to good use during the year.

LACY CROCHET TOTE BAG

Average: For those with some experience in crocheting.

Materials: J. & P. Coats Knit-Cro-Sheen (250-yard ball): 4 balls of Ecru; size 8 steel crochet hook, OR ANY SIZE HOOK TO OBTAIN GAUGE BELOW; stitch markers; tapestry needle.
Gauge: 4 spaces = 1 inch.
Note: *The tote bag is made in rounds. The bottom of the tote is made last, and stitched to the side and back panels. The shell trim and handles are added after the tote is finished.*

Directions:
1. Panels: Starting at the bottom, ch 272. ***Rnd 1:*** Ch 4 (counts as dc and ch-1), *skip 1-ch, dc in next ch-1 — **sp made*** (place a marker in this space); * ch 1, skip 1-ch, dc in next ch; rep from * 11 times more, place a marker; make 56 spaces, place a marker; make 12 spaces, place a marker; end ch 1, join with sl st in third ch of ch-4. You will have 13 spaces from marker to marker, and 55 spaces between — 136 spaces in all. ***Rnd 2:*** *Ch 4, dc in dc — **starting space made;*** ch 1, skip 1-ch, dc in next dc all around. End with sl st in third ch of ch-4.
Rnds 3 to 62: Follow the chart in FIG. V, 6. To make a block, dc in ch-1 sp.

Rnd 63: Ch 1, * sc in dc, sc in ch-1 sp; rep from * around. **Rnds 64 to 69:** Rep Rnd 63. Break off and fasten.

2. Bottom: Attach the thread to the front panel marker, and work across 55 spaces only. Make 12 more rows of 55 spaces. Break the thread. Sew the Bottom to the side and back panels, being careful to sew space for space.

3. Shell Trim: With the bag upside down, starting at the upper left marker, * sc, ch 2, 3 dc, skip 1 sp; rep from * around the filet flower panel. Repeat for the other filet flower panel.

4. Handles (make 2), Row 1: Ch 101. Sc in 2nd ch from hook, sc in each ch across — 100 sc. Ch 1, turn.

Rows 2 to 10: Sc in each sc across. Ch 1, turn; **do not** ch 1 at the end of Row 10. **Row 11:** Fold the handle in half lengthwise. Sl st into first sc on the other side of the fold. Ch 1, * sc through both sides; rep from * around — 100 sc. Fasten off.

5. Finishing: Using the photo *(page 120)* as a placement guide, center and sew the handles to the front and back flower panels.

FIG. V, 6 LACY CROCHET TOTE BAG

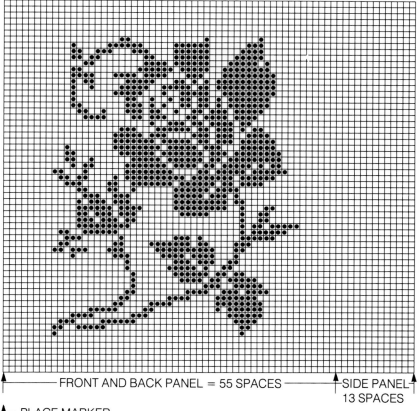

|← ——— FRONT AND BACK PANEL = 55 SPACES ——— →|← SIDE PANEL →|
13 SPACES

↑ = PLACE MARKER
WORK ACROSS DESIGN 2 TIMES — 136 SPACES

TIPS FOR A "GREEN" CHRISTMAS

Green Bagging It!

Some department stores, especially fancy ones, wrap purchases in tissue paper, pack them in a small bag, and put the bag in a handled shopping bag. That's a lot of paper wasted.

Instead, ask the store clerk to put your purchase in a handled shopping bag without any other wrapping. Then use the large bag to hold your other purchases — no extra paper needed!

JUST FOR HIM

A choice selection of perfect presents for the
special men in your life.

MOUNTAIN SCENE MARQUETRY BOX

(7 x 4½ x 3 inches)

Marquetry is the art of creating inlaid scenic pictures from wood veneers in the style of a jigsaw puzzle. The varieties of wood suggested below can be replaced with others that appeal to you more, or that you happen to have on hand. The grain, color, and feel of the wood varieties used are integral parts of the scene.

Challenging: Requires more experience in crafting.

Materials: ¼ x 36 x 4-inch walnut or other hardwood board; veneer sheets: cherry, Carpathian elm burl, ebony, mahogany, maple, oak, green poplar burl, purpleheart, satinwood, walnut and walnut butt; 6½ x 4 inches of velvet or felt; two ¾-inch brass butt hinges; wood glue; white glue; contact cement; rubber cement; rubber cement thinner *(optional)*; cotton swabs *(optional)*; 100, 150 and 220 grit sandpaper; sanding block; No. 0000 steel wool; tack cloth; fine sawdust; Deft Interior Satin Finish; paste wax *(optional)*; clean soft cloth *(optional)*; paintbrush; scissors; small putty knife; craft knife; straight edge; power saw, or handsaw; fret saw, or scroll saw; backsaw; No. 4/0 (jeweler's) saw blades; miter box; router; screwdriver; band clamp; parallel clamp or vise; 2 boards for clamping; corrugated cardboard; sheet of oaktag paper; wax paper; carbon paper; paper for patterns.

Note: *The veneer sheets can be ordered from: Craftman Wood Service Co., 1735 West Cortland Ct., Addison, IL 60101; Bob Morgan Woodworking Supplies, 1123 Bardstown Road, Louisville, KY 40204; Constantine's, 2050 Eastchester Rd., Bronx, NY 10461.*

Directions:

1. Trace the full-size inlay pattern in FIG. V, 7A *(page 125)* onto paper. Make three exact copies of the pattern. Spread out the veneers and two copies of the pattern, along with the scissors, craft knife and rubber cement. Use the key in FIG. V, 7A and the photo as guides to select the veneer to use for each scene part.

2. Starting with one of the smallest scene parts, such as a tree trunk or bush, cut out a piece of veneer slightly larger than the scene part. Cut the piece so the wood grain goes in a direction that enhances the scene; the arrows on the pattern in FIG. V, 7A suggest the direction of the grain for some scene parts. Glue the piece of veneer in place on one pattern sheet, making sure the scene part is covered completely. Continue to cover scene parts on the pattern sheet in this way, progressing from the smallest to the largest scene parts, and looking for interesting grains or patterns in the veneers to make the scene come alive. After a while, you will begin to cover the lines of other scene parts on the pattern sheet, making it difficult to work accurately. At that point, begin gluing veneer pieces onto the second pattern sheet. It doesn't matter which pattern sheet the veneer pieces are glued onto, as long as all the scene parts are covered completely.

3. When all the scene parts are covered with veneer pieces, cut a piece of corrugated cardboard the same size as the pattern sheets. Line up the two pattern sheets carefully, and place them on the cardboard. Place the third pattern sheet on top. Glue the cardboard and the pattern sheets together by spreading rubber cement over the entire surface of each sheet. Making sure the sheets are lined up exactly, clamp the pattern sandwich between the two clamping boards, and let the glue dry overnight.

4. Use the fret saw or scroll saw with a No. 4/0 blade for the final cutting of the veneer scene pieces. Cut out each scene piece carefully, one piece at a time, sawing through the entire sandwich at once as you work. Two or more veneer pieces are likely to have overlapped in the gluing process, so separate the papers of each scene part gently until you find the veneer piece cut in the correct shape. When you have cut and removed all the veneer scene pieces, discard the remainder of the sandwich.

5. To assemble the veneer pieces into the scene, spread a thin layer of rubber cement on the oaktag. Place the largest veneer piece, the oak sky, face down on the oaktag. Place an adjacent veneer piece, such as the purpleheart mountain, face down in place against the oak sky. Continue in this way until all the veneer pieces are assembled into the scene. Let the rubber cement dry for a few minutes. Using 100 grit sandpaper, sand off any excess rubber cement that is on the back of the veneer scene, which is the side facing up. Or, if you wish, use rubber cement thinner very sparingly on a cotton swab to remove the rubber cement.

6. Mix some fine sawdust with white glue to a putty-like consistency. Using the putty knife, push the sawdust putty into any gaps or imperfections in the veneer scene. Wipe off any excess putty.

7. Cut two 7 x 3-inch pieces, and two 4⅜ x 3-inch pieces from the walnut or other hardwood board for the box sides. Miter their ends 45°. Rabbet a ¼-inch groove on the inside top and bottom edges of each box side *(see FIG. V, 7B, page 125)*. Glue the sides together with wood glue, band clamp them, and let the glue dry overnight.

8. Cut two 6¾ x 4⅛-inch pieces from the walnut board for the box top and bottom. Glue the top and bottom into the rabbet joints in the box sides, clamp the top and bottom in place, and let the glue dry overnight. Progressing from 100 grit to 220 grit sandpaper, sand the box top and bottom smooth. Wipe off all the sawdust with the tack cloth.

9. Following the package directions, spread a thin layer of contact cement on the box top, and on the back of the veneer scene. Let the contact cement dry. Coat the box top and back of the scene again. Centering the veneer scene carefully on the box top, attach the scene to the box top by pressing hard and evenly on the scene to assure good contact and remove air bubbles. Peel off the oaktag.

10. Using the craft knife, cut the ebony veneer into ⅟₁₆-inch-wide strips to go around the perimeter of the veneer scene. Cut the Carpathian elm burl veneer into ½-inch-wide strips to go around the ebony strips *(see* Fig. V, 7A*)*. Coat the top edges of the box and one side of the veneer strips with contact cement. Let the contact cement dry. Coat the box top and veneer strips again. Place a small piece of wax paper on each corner of the box top, overlapping the box edges. Press the veneer strips in place; they will overlap each other at the corners. At one corner, use the straight edge and craft knife to cut down to the box top through all the veneer strip layers from the corner of the scene to the corner of the box, creating a 45° miter *(see photo, page 122)*. Peel off and discard the scrap veneer pieces. Slip out the wax paper, and press the mitered strips against the box top; they should fit together tightly. Repeat at the other corners.

11. Using 100 grit sandpaper on the sanding block, sand the veneered box top very carefully. Sand just until the scene and border seem level and smooth; the veneer is only ⅟₂₈ inch thick. Then sand carefully with 150 grit sandpaper, and finish with 220 grit sandpaper.

12. Brush the veneered box top with four very heavy coats of Satin Finish, allowing 1 day's drying time between coats. After the fourth coat, sand the box top with 150 grit sandpaper until the surface is level. Wipe off the dust with the tack cloth. Check that the finish has coated the veneered scene evenly. Touch up any uneven spots, and let them dry. Give the box top a final heavy coat of finish, and let it dry for at least 1 week.

13. While the veneered top is drying and hardening, complete the box. Measure down 1 inch from the top of the box, and cut through the entire box *(see* Fig. V, 7B*)*. Attach the brass hinges to the top and bottom sections of the box at the back. Sand the box sides smooth, progressing from 100 to 220 grit sandpaper, and wipe off all the sawdust with the tack cloth. Brush the box sides with three very thin coats of finish, allowing 1 day's drying time between coats.

14. When the box has dried completely, sand it lightly with 220 grit sandpaper. For a satin finish, rub the entire box lightly with the steel wool. For a gloss finish, apply a coat of paste wax with a clean soft cloth after rubbing with the steel wool. Attach the velvet or felt to the inside bottom of the box with rubber cement, rolling under the edges of the velvet as you glue.

15. Dust the box regularly, and rub it periodically with a soft cloth to remove fingerprints. To remove scratches or dirt stains, rub them with No. 0000 steel wool in the direction of the wood grain.

FIG. V, 7A MOUNTAIN SCENE MARQUETRY BOX INLAY   FULL SIZE

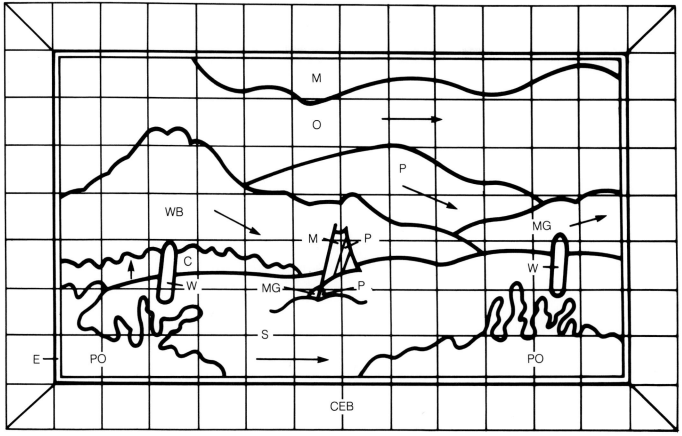

ARROWS = GRAIN DIRECTION

C = CHERRY
CEB = CARPATHIAN
        ELM BURL
E = EBONY
M = MAPLE
MG = MAHOGANY
O = OAK
P = PURPLEHEART
PO = POPLAR BURL
S = SATINWOOD
W = WALNUT
WB = WALNUT BUTT

FIG. V, 7B BOX

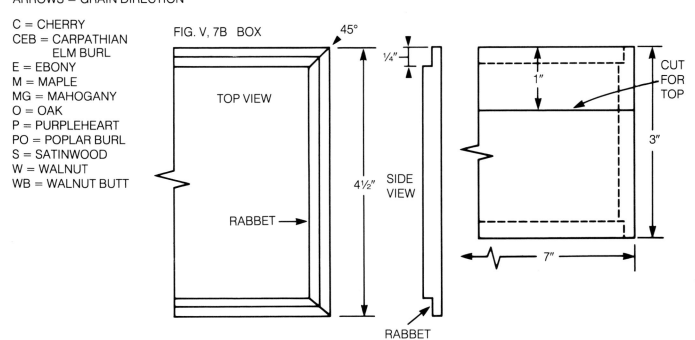

CLEVER CRAFTING

Dyed in the Wool

Check the dye lots on the yarn you use for sweaters, afghans and other large knitted or crocheted projects. Make sure all skeins of the same color come from the same dye lot. The slightest variation in color or shade will be noticeable in the finished project.

MAN'S V-NECK CARDIGAN

Challenging: Requires more experience in knitting.

Directions are given for Size Small. Changes for Sizes Medium and Large are in parentheses.

Materials: Knitting worsted weight yarn: 33 (36, 40) ounces of color desired; matching sewing thread; 6 decorative buttons in matching color; 1 pair each size 6, size 7, and size 9 knitting needles, OR ANY SIZE NEEDLES TO OBTAIN GAUGE BELOW; cable needle; stitch holder; stitch markers; tapestry needle; sewing needle.

Gauge: On size 9 needles in Pattern Stitch I, 14 sts = 2½ inches; 6 rows = 1 inch. On size 9 needles in Stockinette Stitch (st st), 3¾ sts = 1 inch; 5 rows = 1 inch. On size 7 needles in Pattern Stitch II, 9 sts = 2 inches; 8 rows = 1 inch.

Buttonhole, Row 1: Work first 4 sts of the Edge Band, bind off next 4 sts, work rem 4 sts. **Row 2:** Work first 4 sts, cast on 4 sts, work rem 4 sts.

Pattern Stitch I: Worked as a multiple of 7 sts plus 1 st, plus 1 selvage st at each edge. **Rows 1, 3 and 5:** K 1, p 1, * (**) slip next 2 sts to cable needle, hold in back of work, k 1, k 2 off cable needle, slip next st to cable needle, hold in front of work, k 2, k 1 off cable needle (**), p 1, k 6, p 1 *; rep from * to * (even multiples of 7) to last st, end k 1; (odd multiples of 7) to last 8 sts, end rep from (**) to (**) over 7 sts, k 1. **Row 2 and all wrong side rows:** K the knit sts and p the purl sts. **Rows 7, 9 and 11:** K 1, p 1, * k 6, p 1, work (**) to (**) of 1st row, p 1 *; rep from * to * (even multiples of 7) to last st, end k 1; (odd multiples of 7) to last 8 sts, end k 6, p 1, k 1. **Row 12:** Rep Row 2. Rep Rows 1 to 12 for pattern.

Pattern Stitch II (worked over odd number of sts), Row 1 (wrong side): Knit. **Row 2:** K 1, * p 1, k 1 *; rep from * to * to end. Rep Rows 1 and 2 for pattern.

Finished Measurements (Blocked):

SIZES:	SMALL	MEDIUM	LARGE
CHEST:	47″	50″	53″

Directions:

1. Back: With size 6 needles, loosely cast on 107 (115, 121) sts. Work in k 1, p 1 ribbing for 2 inches, ending with a right side row. Change to size 9 needles, and work the following foundation row on the wrong side, increasing 1 st for sizes S and L: P 1, k 1, * p 6, k 1 *; rep from * to * to last st, p 1. Start with Row 1 of Pattern Stitch I on the next row, and work even in Pat until total length measures 26 (26½, 27) inches. Bind off in Pat.

2. Left Front: The Left Front is worked with the Edge Band attached, and 6 buttonholes made in the Band at ¾ (1, 1) inch, 3¼ (3½, 3½) inches, 5¾ (6, 6) inches, 8 (8½, 8¾) inches, 10½ (11, 11¼) inches, and 13 (13½, 14) inches. With size 6 needles, loosely cast on 61 (63, 67) sts. Work in k 1, p 1 ribbing for 2 inches, making the first buttonhole at ¾ (1, 1) inch. End with a right side row. Change to size 9 needles, and work p 1, k 1 ribbing over the first 12 sts, then work the following foundation row over the remaining sts, increasing 1 st for sizes M and L: S and L (k 2, p 3, k 1); M (k 2); * p 6, k 1 *; rep from * to * to last st, p 1 — 61 (64, 68) sts. Start with Row 1 of Pattern Stitch I on the next row, working extra sts after Pat repeats in k or p as established, and working k 1, p 1 ribbing over the Edge Band sts. Continue to work Pat over Pat sts, and ribbing over ribbing sts while making buttonholes at the appropriate measurements, and skipping the Edge Band sts for 2 rows every 12 rows as follows: Work across

Pat sts on right side row, bring yarn to front, slip next st to right needle, bring yarn to back, slip the slipped st on right needle back to the left needle, turn work and work across Pat sts on wrong side to end of row. Work until the total length measures 13½ (14, 14½) inches. Place a marker.

3. V-Neck Shaping: On the next row decrease 1 st over the 2 Pat sts that are just next to the 12 Edge Band sts. (The shaping is done over the Pat sts, not over the Edge Band sts.) Rep on the next row. Then decrease 1 st over these 2 sts every 5th row 13 (14, 14) times more. When the total length measures 26 (26½, 27) inches, bind off Pat sts in Pat, and place the Edge Band sts on the st holder.

4. Right Front: The Right Front is worked without an Edge Band. The Edge Band will be worked later from the sts on the Left Front holder and sewn to the Right Front. With size 6 needles, loosely cast on 49 (53, 57) sts. Work in k 1, p 1 ribbing for 2 inches, ending with a right side row. Change to size 9 needles and work the following foundation row, increasing 1 st for size S: P 1, k 1, * p 6, k 1 *; rep from * to * 5 (6, 6) times more, work S and L (p 3, k 3), M (k 3) over rem sts — 50 (53, 57) sts. On the next row work Row 1 of Pat Stitch I as follows: S (p 3, k 3, p 1, * k 6, p 1, work cabling over next 6 sts, p 1 *; rep from * to * to last st, k 1); M (p 3, k 6, p 1, * work cabling over next 6 sts, p 1, k 6, p 1 *; rep from * to * to last st, k 1); L (p 3, k 3, p 1, work cabling over next 6 sts, p 1, * k 6, p 1, work cabling over next 6 sts, p 1 *; rep from * to * to last st, k 1). Continue working in Pat as established, working the extra sts after the Pat repeats in k or p as established. Work until the total length measures 13½ (14, 14½) inches — the same row as the marker on the Left Front.

5. V-Neck Shaping: On the next row, decrease 1 st over the 2 sts at the center edge. Rep on the next row. Then decrease these 2 sts every 5th row 13 (14, 14) times more. When the total length measures 26 (26½, 27) inches, the same as the Left Front, bind off in Pat.

6. Sleeves: With size 6 needles, loosely cast on 49 (51, 53) sts. Work in k 1, p 1 ribbing for 2 inches, ending with a right side row. Change to size 9 needles and work the following foundation row, increasing 22 (22, 24) sts evenly spaced: S (k 1); M (p 1, k 1); L (p 3, k 1); * p 6, k 1 *; rep from * to * to S (end); M (last st, p 1); L (last 3 sts, p 3). Work Row 1 of Pat Stitch I as follows: S (p 1); M (k 1, p 1); L (k 3, p 1), * k 6, p 1, work cabling over next 6 sts, p 1 *; rep from * to * to S (end); M (last st, k 1); L (last 3 sts, k 3). Continue working Pat as established, working the extra sts at the edges as established. When total length measures 2½ inches, increase 1 st at each edge every 5th row 15 (16, 16) times. When increasing, expand the Pat appropriately, working the cables in half or whole only when there are at least 2 edge sts. When the total length measures 15½ (16, 16) inches, end with a wrong side row. Change to size 7 needles, and k the knit sts and p the purl sts for 3 rows. Then work Pattern Stitch II for 3 (3, 3½) inches — the total length will measure 19 (19½, 20) inches. Bind off. Sew the Shoulder seams.

7. Edge Band: Count the number of ribbing rows worked on size 9 needles (the rows above the waistband). Place a marker on the last row worked. Continue in ribbing as established on size 9 needles. Work a length to loosely fit the back of the Neck, and place a marker. From the second marker, work the same number of rows that you counted on the Left Front. Change to size 6 needles, and work for 2 inches more — the number of rows worked for the waistband. Bind off loosely. Pin the Edge Band to the Right Front and back of the Neck, matching markers to the Shoulder seams. Lay the pieces flat, and sl st them together through half of each edge st.

8. Pockets: Pick up 30 sts evenly spaced over 7 inches of the Back side edge, starting 1 inch above the ribbing. Work in st st (k 1 row, p 1 row; the right side the same as the Back's right side) for 8 inches. Bind off.

9. Finishing: Block the pieces to the finished measurements, and help to shape the V-neck. Sew the side seams from the bottom edge to the beginning of the Pocket and above the Pocket upwards, leaving 11 (11½, 12) inches open for the Sleeve. Sew the Sleeve seams. Sew in the Sleeves. From the outside, pin the Left and Right Front edges in place over the Pockets. Open the Fronts to the inside, and pin the Pockets in place on the Fronts. Using the sewing needle and thread, slipstitch the edges of the Pockets to the Fronts *(see Stitch Guide, page 168)*. Sew the buttons in place.

TRAVELING SLIPPERS WITH CASE

Average: For those with some experience in sewing.

SLIPPERS

Materials: 1 pair of insoles in size required; ½ yard of 45-inch-wide quilted red corduroy fabric; 4 yards of extra-wide black bias tape; black thread; dressmaker's carbon; tracing wheel; tracing paper for pattern.

Directions:

1. Trace the full-size half pattern for the Slipper Top in FIG. V, 8 *(page 130)* onto folded tracing paper. Cut out the half pattern through the double-thickness paper. Open the paper for the full pattern.

2. Using the dressmaker's carbon and tracing wheel, trace two Slipper Tops onto a double thickness of the red corduroy, leaving at least 1 inch between the Tops. The traced lines are the sewing lines; cut ½ inch outside the traced lines to make two pairs of Slipper Tops. Using the insoles as patterns, repeat to cut out two pairs of Slipper Bottoms.

3. Using the photo as a design and placement guide, attach bias tape trim to two Slipper Tops with a machine zigzag stitch.

4. Baste one trimmed Slipper Top to a plain Slipper Top, wrong sides together and edges matching. Using a machine zigzag stitch, bind the two long edges of the double Slipper Top with bias tape. Repeat.

5. Place one pair of Slipper Bottoms wrong sides together, and place the matching insole between them. Machine baste all the layers together. Repeat to make a second complete Slipper Bottom.

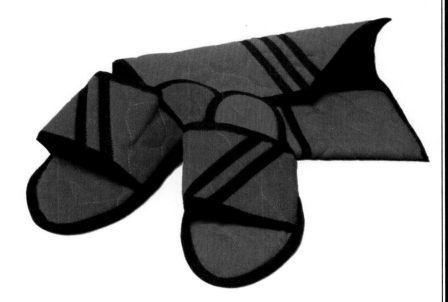

6. Pin a Slipper Top to each Slipper Bottom, with the Top's shorter bound edge facing the Bottom's toe *(see photo)*. Try on each Slipper, and adjust the Top's position for comfort if necessary. Machine baste the raw side edges of the Slipper Tops to the Slipper Bottoms.

7. Using a machine zigzag stitch, bind the edges of the Slipper Bottoms with bias tape, lapping the tape over the Slipper Tops' raw side edges.

CASE

Materials: 12½ x 18½ inches of quilted red corduroy fabric; 12½ x 18½ inches of black lining fabric; 3 yards of extra-wide black bias tape; black thread; large snap fastener.

Directions:

1. Fold the corduroy in half lengthwise, raw edges even. Mark the raw long edge 2 inches in from one short end. Draw a line from the mark to the end of the folded long edge on the same side. Cut along the drawn line through both layers of fabric to shape the case flap. Repeat on the lining fabric.

2. Pin a strip of bias tape across the lengthwise center of the case, and machine zigzag stitch along each edge of the tape. Pin and zigzag stitch a strip of bias tape ⅜ inch from each side of the center tape *(see photo)*.

3. With wrong sides together, pin and machine baste the lining to the corduroy. Bind the straight end of the case with a 12½-inch-long strip of bias tape. Fold the bound end 5½ inches up, and pin the side edges together.

4. Bind the case side edges with bias tape, folding under the tape's raw ends. Repeat on the case flap edges, mitering the tape at the corners.

5. Sew half the snap fastener to the underside of the flap, and the other half to a corresponding position on the case front.

TIPS FOR A "GREEN" CHRISTMAS

Recycled Wrapping

Just about every kind of gift wrap, including aluminum foil gift wrap, can be recycled. However, some types of wrapping paper are more difficult and more costly to process than others. Before you invest in yards and yards of Christmas wrapping, ask your local paper recyclers what kinds of paper they process. Then you can choose your gift wraps accordingly.

According to Bob Patterson, spokesman for Automated Materials Handling, a Kensington, Connecticut recycler, most household paper is recycled into two forms: newsprint and boxboard. Newsprint, used for printing newspapers, is made almost exclusively from old newspapers. Boxboard—a lightweight cardboard used for such things as tissue boxes, pizza boxes and shirt cardboard—is made from old newspapers, magazines, junk mail, phone books, and other low-grade paper. Used wrapping paper can be processed into boxboard.

If you're still unsure about what kind of paper to use for your Christmas wrapping, try newspaper! With a little imagination, you can turn the daily paper into newsworthy gift wrap.

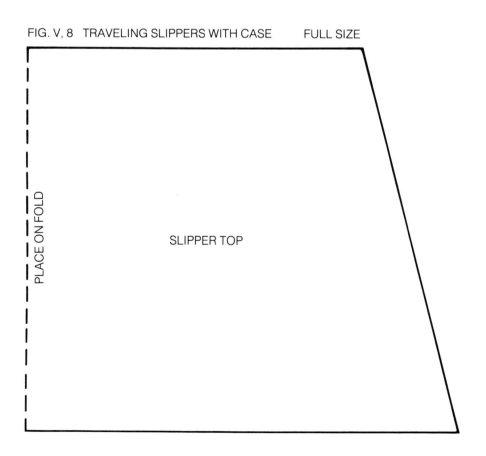

FIG. V, 8   TRAVELING SLIPPERS WITH CASE   FULL SIZE

PLACE ON FOLD

SLIPPER TOP

Toiletries Rack; Shower Shelf (directions, page 133)

TOILETRIES RACK

Average: For those with some experience in woodworking.

Materials: 6 feet of 1 x 4 clear pine lumber; 12 feet of ½ x ½-inch pine ballister; ¾-inch brads; wood glue; wood putty; sandpaper; tack cloth; satin polyurethane; paintbrush; saw; hammer; nail set.

Directions:

1. Cut, rabbet and notch the A top and bottom shelves, B long shelf, and C short shelves *(see Cutting Directions and* FIG. V, 9, *page 132)*. Cut the D supports and E short supports to size.
2. Glue and nail the C short shelves and B long shelf to the D supports and E short supports. Glue and nail the A top and bottom shelves in place *(see* FIG. V, 9*)*. Check that all is square.
3. Set the nails, and fill the nail holes with wood putty. When the putty is dry, sand it. Sand the rack smooth, and wipe off all the sawdust with the tack cloth. Apply three coats of polyurethane, sanding the rack lightly between coats.

TIPS FOR A "GREEN" CHRISTMAS

Twice as Nice Cards

Cut the front panels off old Christmas cards to make holiday postcards. It's a great way to reuse the cards you received last year, and a smart way to salvage cards when you've run out of envelopes or made a writing mistake. Your ingenuity will cut down on paper waste, and you'll save on holiday postage costs.

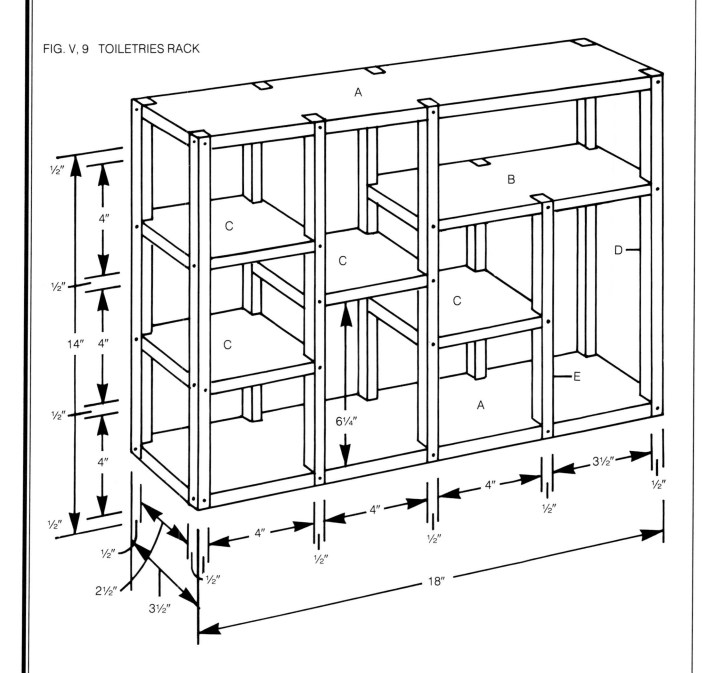

FIG. V, 9 TOILETRIES RACK

Cutting Directions

Code	Pieces	Size
A	2	½" x 3½" x 18" Top and bottom shelves
B	1	½" x 3½" x 9" Long shelf
C	4	½" x 3½" x 5" Short shelves
D	8	½" x ½" x 14" Supports
E	2	½" x ½" x 9½" Short supports

132

SHOWER SHELF

(photo, page 131)

Average: For those with some experience in woodworking.

Materials: 1 x 5 clear pine lumber; ⅜-inch-diameter wooden dowels; ¼-inch-diameter nylon rope; sandpaper; tack cloth; exterior marine grade polyurethane; paintbrush; saw; power bore, or power drill.

Directions:

1. Cut two 8½-inch lengths from the pine lumber. On the long front edge of each length, mark 1½ inches up from the bottom. On the top edge, mark in 1½ inches from the back. Connect the marks, and cut on the line. Sand all the corners round to make the shelf sides.

2. On one shelf side, measure ¾ inch O.C. from the back edge, and mark the positions for four dowels 1 inch apart and ¾ inch from the bottom edge. Three inches O.C. above the lower positions, mark three more dowel positions to align with the back three lower marks.

3. Drill a ⅜-inch-diameter hole at each marked position; a power bore will work best. Also drill a ¼-inch-diameter rope hole 1 inch from the top and ¾ inch from the back edge of the shelf side.

4. Use the drilled shelf side to mark the hole positions on the second shelf side; drill the holes. Cut seven 6⅞-inch-long dowels, and insert them into the shelf sides flush with the sides' outer edges.

5. Sand the shelf smooth, and wipe off all the sawdust with the tack cloth. Apply three coats of polyurethane, sanding lightly between coats. Let the polyurethane dry completely.

6. Thread a 4-inch length of nylon rope through the rope holes from the inside to the outside of the shelf, and knot the ends of the rope *(see photo)*.

CLEVER CRAFTING

Potato-Stamp Wrap

Kids love to make potato-stamp gift wrap. Depending on the age of the child, you can cut the stamps for them or let them create their own stamps.

Cut a potato in half across the width. Pencil a simple shape on the cut surface of each potato half, or use Christmas cookie cutters for patterns. Use a kitchen paring knife to cut away the potato around each design, leaving a raised area that will be the stamp.

Test the potato stamps by pressing them on an ink stamp pad, and then on a piece of scrap paper. Adjust the stamp designs, if necessary. Try different combinations of shapes and colored inks, but use only one ink color on each stamp.

Spread plain brown paper on a flat surface (the unprinted sides of grocery bags work well for this), and let the kids stamp on the designs. Colored wide felt tip markers can be used to add zigzags, dotted lines, and stars around the stamped designs.

The kids also can make stamped ribbons for bows. Cut brown paper into strips of various lengths, and let the kids stamp them. Bend the ends of each strip to meet in the middle, and secure the ends with tape. Stack strip loops on top of each other in order of size, with the largest at the bottom. Wind a short brown paper strip around the loops in the middle, and secure the strip with tape.

TIPS FOR A "GREEN" CHRISTMAS

Set for Green Business

Anyone who works at a desk, including a college student, will appreciate receiving an attractive set of desk accessories as a Christmas gift. Make sure the set includes a refillable pen and pencil, and a desk-top adhesive tape dispenser. These reusable items reduce the need for disposable pens, wooden pencils, and throwaway plastic tape dispensers.

THE KIDS' CORNER

Surprise your special children with
wondrous toys, snuggly sweaters, winter-
warm mittens, or a hand-painted rocking
chair just their size!

WINTER WONDERLAND SWEATERS & HATS

Average: For those with some experience in knitting.

Directions are given for Child's Size 2. Changes for Sizes 4 and 6 are in parentheses.

Materials: Melrose Woolympia yarn (2-ounce skein): 3 (3, 4) skeins of Navy for each sweater, and 1 skein of Navy for each hat; Lion Brand Molaine yarn (40-gram ball): 1 ball each of Red and White; Lion Brand Angora yarn (10-gram ball): 1 ball of Green; 1 pair each size 6 and size 8 knitting needles, OR ANY SIZE NEEDLES TO OBTAIN GAUGE BELOW; 4 stitch holders; stitch markers; tapestry needle; 3-inch cardboard square.

Gauge: On size 8 needles in Stockinette Stitch (st st), 4 sts = 1 inch; 6 rows = 1 inch.

Note: *The tree or snowman motif is worked in duplicate stitch when the sweater is completed.*

SWEATER

Measurements:

SIZES:	2	4	6
BODY CHEST:			
	21"	23"	25"

Finished Measurements:

CHEST:	23"	25"	27"
WIDTH ACROSS BACK OR FRONT AT UNDERARMS:			
	11½"	12½"	13½"
WIDTH ACROSS SLEEVE AT UPPER ARM:			
	8½"	9"	9½"

Directions:

1. Back: With size 6 needles and Navy, cast on 45 (49, 53) sts.

Ribbing, Row 1 (wrong side): P 1, * k 1, p 1; rep from * across. ***Row 2:*** K 1, * p 1, k 1; rep from * across. Work even in ribbing for 2 inches, ending with Row 1; inc 1 st at end of last row. Continue in st st (k 1 row, p 1 row) with size 8 needles on 46 (50, 54) sts until 6 (6½, 7) inches above ribbing, or desired length to underarm, ending with a p row.

2. Raglan Armhole Shaping: Bind off 2 sts at beg of next 2 rows. ***Dec Row:*** K 1, sl 1, k 1, psso, k across until 3 sts rem, k 2 tog, k 1. P 1 row, k 1 row, p 1 row. Rep Dec Row on next row, then every other row until 20 sts remain. Sl sts to a st holder.

3. Front: Work as for the Back until 3 inches above beg of Armhole Shaping. Mark center 12 sts.

4. Neck Shaping: Continuing to work Raglan dec as for the Back, work to first marker, with 2nd strand of yarn, work to next marker, sl center 12 sts to another st holder, work to end. Working each side separately, dec 1 st at each Neck edge on next row, then every other row 3 times more. Continue Raglan dec until 1 st rem. Fasten off.

5. Sleeves: With size 6 needles and Navy, cast on 23 (25, 27) sts. Work in ribbing as for the Back, inc 1 st on last row—24 (26, 28) sts. Change to size 8 needles. Work even in st st for 1 inch. If desired, stripes can be knitted now for the Trees sweater as follows: Work 2 rows of Red, 6 rows of Navy, 2 rows of Red, working incs as indicated. Keeping in st st, inc 1 st each edge on next row, then every 1 inch 4 times more—34 (36, 38) sts. Work even until the Sleeves are 8½ (10½, 11½) inches from beg, or desired length to underarm.

6. Raglan Cap Shaping: Bind off 2 sts at beg of next 2 rows. Dec 1 st at each edge for Back on next row, then every other row 11 (13, 15) times more. Sl rem 6 (4, 2) sts to a st holder.

7. Finishing: Pin the pieces to the finished measurements, dampen the pieces, and let them dry. Sew the left Sleeve to the Back and Front. Sew the right Sleeve to the Front *only.*

8. Neckband: With the right side facing and size 6 needles, k across sts on the Back holder, k sts from the Sleeves, pick up and k 9 (13, 16) sts to the Front holder, k sts from the holder, pick up and k 10 (14, 17) sts to the end—63 (67, 69) sts. Work even in ribbing as for the Back for 4 rows. Bind off in ribbing.

9. Embroidery: Following the chart in FIG. V, 10A or 10B *(page 136)*, work the Trees or Snowman design in duplicate st *(see Stitch Guide, page 168)*. Using the photo as a placement guide, work snowflakes in White straight stitch, and flowers in Red straight stitch. Work the Snowman's mouth in Green straight stitch. Work Navy French knots for the Snowman's eyes and buttons *(see Stitch Guide)*.

10. Finishing: Sew side and Sleeve seams. Sew right Sleeve to the Back.

HAT
Directions:

1. With size 6 needles and Navy, cast on 67 sts. Work in k 1, p 1 ribbing as for the Back for 23 rows; if desired, beg stripe pat on 7th row and work following Step 5. Change to size 8 needles and st st, and work even until 6½ inches above ribbing. ***First Dec Row:*** K 1, * k 2 tog, k 8; rep from * across, end last rep with k 4. Work 1 row even. ***Second Dec Row:*** * K 2 tog, k 8; rep from * across. Work 1 row even. ***Third Dec Row:*** * K 2 tog, k 7; rep from * across. Work 1 row even. ***Fourth Dec Row:*** * K 2 tog, k 6; rep from * across. Work 1 row even. ***Fifth Dec Row:*** * K 2 tog, k 5; rep from * across. For the shorter Hat, work even on 36 sts for 3 inches. For the longer Hat, work even for 6 inches, work 2 rows of Red, work 2 inches of Navy. ***Last Row:*** K 2 tog across. Cut the yarn, leaving a 12-inch end. Thread the yarn through the remaining sts, and draw up tightly. Fasten securely. Sew the back seam, taking care to sew the seam at the cuff on the wrong side.

2. Pompon: Wrap yarn around the cardboard. Slip a separate strand under the yarn at one end, and knot the strand securely. Cut the yarn at the other end. Fasten the pompon to the top of the Hat.

FIG. V, 10A TREES

CENTER

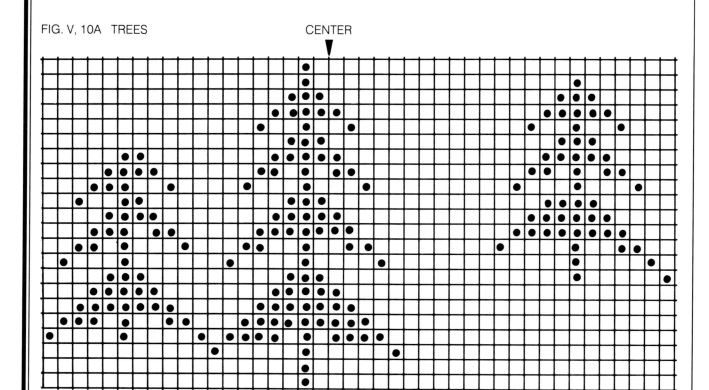

● = WHITE

CENTER

FIG. V, 10B SNOWMAN

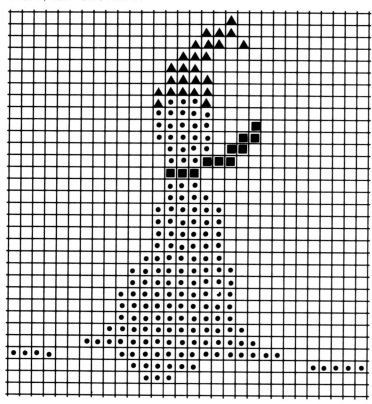

■ = RED   ▲ = GREEN   ● = WHITE

MITTEN MAGIC

Average: For those with some experience in knitting.

Directions given for Size 6-7 Years.
Materials: Worsted weight yarn: about 2 ounces of main color (MC), and scraps of other colors indicated for design of your choice in Fig. V, 11A or 11B *(page 138)*; four size 5 double-pointed knitting needles (dp), OR ANY SIZE NEEDLES TO OBTAIN GAUGE BELOW; 2 stitch holders; 4 bobbins; 4 stitch stoppers, or rubber bands; tapestry needle.
Gauge: In Stockinette Stitch (st st), 5 sts = 1 inch; 6½ rows = 1 inch.
Directions:
1. First Mitten: Begin the Mitten on 2 needles. Place the stitch stoppers or rubber bands on the ends of the

needles to keep the stitches from falling off. With MC, cast on 30 sts, and work in k 1, p 1 ribbing for 14 rows. Start st st (k 1 row, p 1 row) and the design, following the chart in Fig. V, 11A or 11B, on **Row 15,** inc 4 sts evenly; odd numbers are knit rows. Work Santa's beard using 1 bobbin. Work each Reindeer leg with 1 piece of yarn without using a bobbin. Work through Row 20. ***Thumb Increase, Row 21:*** K 16, inc 1 in each of next 2 sts, k 16. ***Row 22:*** P. ***Row 23:*** K 16, inc 1 in next st, k 2, inc 1 in next st, k 16. ***Row 24:*** P. ***Row 25:*** K 16, inc 1 in next st, k 4, inc 1 in next st, k 16. ***Row 26:*** P. Keep inc in this manner, with 2 more sts between incs each time, and work a p row between inc rows. When you have 10 sts between incs, p one more row. ***Next Row:*** K 17, and put on a st holder, k across 12 sts for thumb, and put rem 17 sts

on another st holder. Divide the thumb sts on 3 needles, remove the stoppers, and work around 9 rnds evenly. ***Next Rnd:*** * K 1, k 2 tog; rep from * around. ***Next Rnd:*** Work 2 tog across. Run yarn through sts, pull up and fasten off. Slip first sts from holder to right needle, last to left needle. Tie in yarn in front of left needle. Picking up 1 st at base of thumb, work with 2 needles across the last sts and continue to end of chart. ***Row 45:*** * K 1, k 2 tog, k 12, sl 1, k 1, psso; rep from * across. ***Row 46:*** P. ***Row 47:*** * K 1, k 2 tog, k 10, sl 1, k 1, psso; rep from * across. ***Row 48:*** P. Continue like this for 2 more dec rows and 2 more p rows. Divide rem sts equally between 2 needles, and weave top together.
2. Santa, Face: With pale pink, cast on 3 sts, work 2 rows st st, bind off, and sew into a ball. Sew the ball to

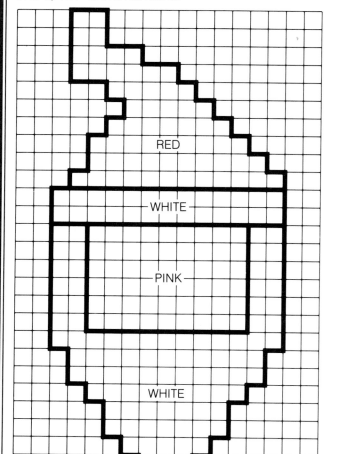

RED

WHITE

PINK

WHITE

GREEN

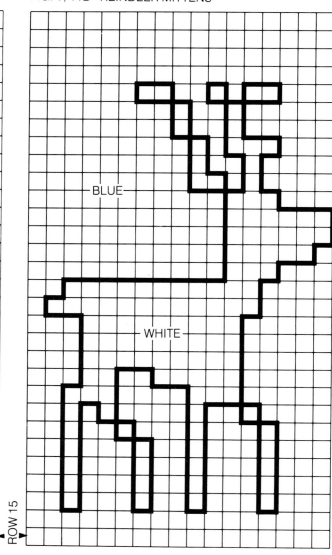

BLUE

WHITE

ROW 15

Santa's face for a nose. Work Santa's eyes in blue straight stitch *(see Stitch Guide, page 168, and photo, page 137)*. **Pompon:** With white, cast on 5 sts, work 4 rows st st, bind off, and sew into a ball. Sew the ball to the tip of Santa's hat for a pompon.

3. Reindeer: Work the Reindeer's eye with 1 blue French knot, and nose with 1 red French knot. Work 1 red straight stitch for the collar *(see photo and Stitch Guide)*.

4. Second Mitten: Reverse the design, and work it on the other side of the Mitten.

5. Finishing: Sew the side seams using a backstitch. Press the Mittens lightly with a warm steam iron.

FLOWER GIRLS

Make our trio of pretties — Bluebell, Daisy and Rose — to delight any special young girl.

Average: For those with some experience in sewing.

Materials for One Doll: One pastel pink, blue or yellow nylon anklet sock; ¼ yard of 36-inch-wide matching color nylon tulle; 2 yards of ¾-inch-wide matching color nylon lace; 2 ounces of matching color sport yarn; scraps of ⅛-inch-wide matching color ribbon; scraps of matching color embroidery floss, plus Blue and Pink if necessary; matching color and white sewing threads; matching color buttontwist thread; 1 Girls extra-large white cotton sock (shoe size 1-4½); sewing needle; long dollmaking needle; synthetic stuffing; blusher; white glue; strong cardboard.

Directions:

1. Body: Turn the white sock inside out, and lay it flat with the heel up. Pinch up the heel, and fold it toward the toe *(see* FIG. V, 12, *page 140).* Mark, pin and machine-stitch along the solid lines indicated in FIG. V, 12 for the Arms and Legs. Stitch again close to the first rows. Cut apart the Arms and Legs along the broken lines indicated in FIG. V, 12, and trim the seam allowances to ¼ inch. Slit the sock at the toe where indicated in FIG. V, 12, and turn the sock right side out. Stuff the Legs and Body firmly through the slit. Using buttontwist thread, stitch a gathering row around the slit. Pull up the gathers, and fasten the thread securely to close the top of the head.

2. Neck and Arms: Tie a length of buttontwist thread around the Body about 3½ inches from the top of the head to make the neck. Turn the Arms right side out, stuff them, and gather them across their open ends with buttontwist thread. Sew the Arms securely to the Body about ½ inch below the neck.

3. Leotard: Cut off the anklet sock cuff ¾ inch below the ribbing. Tack the front securely to the back at the center top edge of the cuff to make the leotard crotch. Put the leotard on the doll, and roll the leotard's raw edge down around the doll's neck. Tack the leotard to the doll at each shoulder. Cut a 14-inch length of lace, and sew a gathering row with buttontwist thread along the lace's straight long edge. Draw up the thread, wrap the lace twice around one doll shoulder, and sew the lace in place. Repeat on the other doll shoulder. Glue a ribbon choker around the doll's neck over the leotard. Tie a matching color embroidery floss bow around each wrist and ankle, and secure the bows with a drop of glue.

4. Tutu: Cut a 6 x 36-inch tulle strip, and stitch lace along one edge. Fold the strip in half lengthwise to 3 inches. Using buttontwist thread, sew long gathering stitches through both layers down the strip's long center. Gather the tutu, lace edge on top, to fit around the doll's waist. Knot the thread, and glue the knot in place.

5. Braids: Lightly mark a center "part" line on the head from the forehead to the nape of the neck. Cut the yarn into 18-inch-long strands. Center the strands on the head at the "part" line. Starting at the forehead, hand-sew the yarn hair, very close together, to the head along the "part" line. Tie thread around the hair at each side of the head, and tack the ties to the head. Braid the hair below each tie into three braids, and trim the ends evenly. Bend each set of braids upward into a loop, and tie the loop in place with a ribbon bow *(see Blue Doll in photo, page 139).*

6. Short Curls: Wrap the yarn around a 2 x 12-inch cardboard strip; do not cut the yarn. Slide the yarn carefully off the cardboard onto the sewing machine, and stitch down the middle of the yarn. Continue to wrap and stitch yarn until you have a 40-inch-long strip of loops. Lightly mark the hairline around the head. Starting at the back of the head, hand-sew the yarn hair, along its stitch line, across the head from side to side. Tie a ribbon bow around the head for a headband *(see Yellow Doll in photo).*

7. Pony Tail: Wrap the yarn closely around a 4½ x 10-inch cardboard rectangle; do not cut the yarn. Slide the yarn carefully off the cardboard onto the sewing machine, and stitch ⅜ inch from the folds on one side. Lightly mark the hairline around the head. Starting and ending at the nape of the neck, hand-sew the yarn hair along its stitch line to the hairline *(see Pink Doll in photo).* Cut twenty 18-inch-long strands of yarn, and braid or twist them together. Tack

FIG. V, 12 FLOWER GIRLS

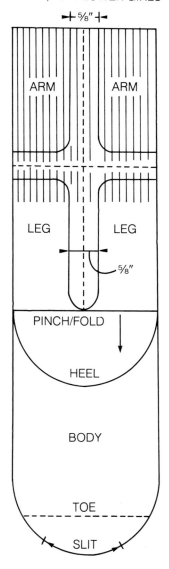

one end of the braid to the top of the head. Gather the yarn hair's loose folded edges around the tacked braid, wrap the loose edges with buttontwist thread, and tie the thread securely. Tie a ribbon bow around the thread.

8. Face: Pin mark the eyes and mouth. Using three strands of floss in the long needle, and entering and exiting through the side of the head to hide the starting and ending knots, work a Pink fly stitch for the mouth, and three Blue French knots for each eye *(see Stitch Guide, page 168).* Pat a little blusher on the doll's cheeks.

BUTTERCUP BABY SET

Average: For those with some experience in crocheting.

Directions given for Size 6 Months.
Materials: Coats & Clark Red Heart® Sofspun Baby Pompadour yarn: 8 ounces of Baby Yellow, and a few yards each of Light Pink, Baby Blue and White; size B crochet hook, OR ANY SIZE HOOK TO OBTAIN GAUGE BELOW; size 7 knitting needle; embroidery floss: ½ yard each of Green and Yellow; 3 yards of ¼-inch-wide yellow ribbon; safety pins; masking tape; tapestry needle; 2 small buttons.
Gauge: 11 ch st = 2 inches; 11 dc = 2 inches; 8 dc rows = 3 inches.

SACQUE
Directions:
1. Right Front Section: The Sacque is worked in one piece. Starting at the Right Front edge with Baby Yellow, ch 51. **Row 1:** Sc in 2nd ch from hook and in next 11 ch for yoke section; place a contrasting color thread between last and next st, and carry up on every row to separate yoke from lower section; dc in each remaining ch — 50 sts. Mark this row for the right side. Ch 3, turn. **Row 2:** Dc in back lp of next dc and in back lp of each dc to thread marker, sc in back lp of each sc across. Ch 1, turn. **Row 3:** Sc in back lp of each sc to thread marker, dc in back lp of each dc to ch-3, dc in top of ch-3. Ch 3, turn. **Rows 4 to 13:** Rep Rows 2 and 3. **Row 14:** Dc in back lp of next 25 dc, do not work over remaining sts — 26 dc counting ch-3 as 1 dc. Ch 3, turn. **Row 15:** Dc in back lp of each dc to ch-3, dc in top of ch-3. Mark last dc worked with a safety pin. Fasten off.
2. Right Sleeve: Starting at Sleeve seam, ch 28. **Row 1 (right side):** Dc in 4th ch from hook and in each ch across — 26 dc counting ch-3 as 1 dc.

Ch 3, turn. **Row 2:** Dc in back lp of next 24 dc, dc in top of ch-3, with wrong side of previous section facing, dc in back lp of first free dc on last long row worked and in back lp of next 11 dc to thread marker, sc in back lp of each sc across—50 sts counting ch-3 as 1 dc. Ch 1, turn. **Row 3:** Rep Row 3 of Right Front Section. **Rows 4 to 17:** Rep Rows 2 and 3 of Right Front Section. **Row 18:** Rep Row 14 of Right Front Section. Fasten off.

3. Back Section: With the wrong side of the Right Front Section facing, join yarn to dc marked with a safety pin. **Joining Row:** Ch 3, dc in back lp of next 25 dc, with wrong side of Sleeve facing, dc in back lp of first free dc on last long row worked and in back lp of each dc to thread marker, sc in back lp of each sc across—50 sts counting ch-3 as 1 dc. Ch 1, turn. **Row 1:** Rep Row 3 of Right Front Section. **Rows 2 to 27:** Rep Rows 2 and 3 of Right Front Section. **Rows 28 to 29:** Rep Rows 14 and 15 of Right Front Section. Fasten off.

4. Left Sleeve: Work as for the Right Sleeve.

5. Left Front Section: With the wrong side of the Back Section facing, join the yarn to the dc marked with a safety pin. **Joining Row:** Work as for Joining Row of Back Section. **Row 1:** Rep Row 3 of Right Front Section. **Rows 2 to 11:** Rep Rows 2 and 3 of Right Front Section. **Row 12:** Rep Row 2 of Right Front Section. Fasten off. Sew the Sleeve and underarm seams.

6. Beading Row: With the right side facing, join the yarn to the Right Front neck corner. **Row 1:** Ch 3, dc in end st of next row and each row along neck edge—86 dc counting ch-3 as 1 dc. Do not turn.

7. Scallop Edging, Rnd 1: Ch 3, dc in base of ch-3, skip ½ inch along Left Front edge, sl st in edge, * ch 3, dc in same place where sl st was made, skip ½ inch along edge, sl st in edge. Rep from * along Left Front edge, lower edge, Right Front edge, and neck

edge. Fasten off. Sew the buttons on 1 Front edge to correspond to the first and third loop of the Scallop Edging on the opposite Front edge.

8. Sleeve Edging: With the right side of the Sleeve facing, join the yarn to the seam at the lower edge. **Rnd 1:** Ch 3, dc in same place where yarn was joined, skip ½ inch along edge, sl st in edge, * ch 3, dc in same place where sl st was made, skip ½ inch along edge, sl st in edge. Rep from * around. Fasten off. Cut a 30-inch length of ribbon, and lace it through the Beading Row, working over 2 dc and under 2 dc across.

9. Flowers: Make 2 Flowers each of Light Pink, Baby Blue and White. Cut a 36-inch length of yarn. Leaving a 3-inch end, tape the yarn lightly to the knitting needle just below the tip. With your left hand, hold the yarn on the needle 3 inches from the tape to form a 6-inch loop. Hold the loop in place with your left thumb. With your right hand, wind the remainder of the yarn 25 times around the needle to cover the taped loop, keeping the wound strand together. Holding the wound strand in place with your left forefinger, remove the tape. Grasp the strands of the taped loop firmly, slip them off the needle, pull them together, and tie them securely. Using the photo on page 141 as a placement guide, sew 1 Flower of each color to the Right Front Section below the yoke. Rep on the Left Front Section. Using the embroidery floss and tapestry needle, work a Yellow French knot at each Flower center. Work leaves around the outer edges of the Flowers in Green lazy daisy stitch *(see Stitch Guide, page 168).*

BOOTIES
Directions:
1. Cuff: Starting at the narrow edge with Baby Yellow, ch 15. **Row 1:** Sc in 2nd ch from hook and in each ch across—14 sc. Ch 1, turn. **Row 2:** Sc

in back lp of each sc across. Ch 1, turn. **Rows 3 to 30:** Rep Row 2. At the end of the last row, ch 1. Do not turn.

2. Lower Section, Rnd 1: Working along the next long edge, sc in end st of each row across. Join with sl st to first sc—30 sc. **Rnds 2 to 4:** Ch 1, sc in joining and in each sc around. Join as before. **Rnd 5:** Ch 1, sc in joining, sc in next 12 sc, mark last st worked with a safety pin, 2 sc in next sc, sc in next 2 sc, 2 sc in next sc, sc in next sc, mark last st worked with a safety pin, sc in each remaining sc around, join—32 sc. Move the safety pins up on every rnd. **Rnd 6:** Sc in joining and in each sc around. Join. **Rnd 7:** Sc in joining and in each sc to marked sc, sc in marked sc, 2 sc in next sc, sc in each sc to 1 sc before next marked sc, 2 sc in next sc, sc in marked sc and in each remaining sc around. Join. There are 2 sc more than on previous rnd. **Rnds 8 to 13:** Rep Rnds 6 and 7—40 sc on last rnd. **Rnd 14:** Ch 1, sc in joining and in each sc around. Join. Fasten off, leaving a 10-inch end for sewing. Fold the lower edge so marked sts are together; sew edges together. Remove safety pins. Sew narrow edges of the cuff together.

3. Tie: Cut two 16-inch lengths of ribbon. Lace a length through the sts on Rnd 2 of each Bootie, weaving over 1 sc and under 1 sc around.

BONNET
Directions:
1. Front Section: Starting at the front edge with Baby Yellow, ch 79. **Row 1:** Dc in 4th ch from hook and in each ch across—76 dc counting ch-3 as 1 dc. Mark this row for the right side of the work. Ch 3, turn. **Rows 2 to 12:** Dc in back lp of next dc and in each dc to ch-3, dc in top of ch-3. Ch 3, turn. Fasten off.

2. Center Back Section, Row 1: With right side facing, skip first 25 dc on previous row, join yarn to next dc, ch 3, dc in back lp of next 25 dc; do not work over remaining sts—26 dc.

Ch 3, turn. **Row 2:** Dc in back lp of next dc and in each dc to ch-3, dc in top of ch-3. Ch 3, turn. **Row 3:** *Holding back on the hook the last lp of each dc, dc in back lp of next 2 dc, yo and draw through all 3 lps on hook—dec made;* dc in back lp of next dc and in each dc to last dc and ch-3, dec over last dc and the ch-3—24 dc. Ch 3, turn. **Rows 4 to 11:** Rep Rows 2 and 3—16 dc on last row. **Row 12:** Rep Row 2. Fasten off. Sew the side edges of Center Back Section to adjacent free sts on Front Section.

3. Scallop Edging: With the right side facing, join the yarn to the lower left front corner of the Bonnet. Working along the neck and front edges, work the Scallop Edging following Sacque, Step 7.

4. Flowers: Make the Flowers following Sacque, Step 9. Sew 1 Flower of each color at each corner of the Bonnet. Embroider the Flower centers and leaves following Sacque, Step 9. Cut a 32-inch length of ribbon, and lace it through the Scallop Edging along the Bonnet neck edge.

RUFFLES & LACE LAYETTE

(photo, page 141; quilt: about 26 x 36 inches, plus ruffle; pillow: 11 inches square, plus ruffle)

Average: For those with some experience in sewing.

QUILT

Materials: 5 feet of 45-inch-wide ivory chintz cotton fabric; 1 yard of 45-inch-wide lace square fabric; 5 yards of 5-inch-wide white ruffled eyelet lace; 12 yards of ¼-inch-wide apricot satin ribbon; apricot and white sewing threads; white buttontwist thread; synthetic batting; large sewing needle; long needle with large eye.

Note: *The directions are based on a lace square fabric with 5¾-inch squares. If fabric with larger or smaller squares is used, the quilt's measurements change accordingly.*

Directions:

1. Cut the lace fabric into a 5-square by 6-square rectangle, or about 28 x 34 inches. Cut two chintz rectangles and two batting rectangles to match. Baste the wrong side of the lace rectangle to the right side of one chintz rectangle. Pin the ruffled eyelet to the lace rectangle right sides together, folding in an extra inch of ruffle at each corner, and having the ruffle's raw ends meet at the center bottom of the rectangle. Using a ¼-inch seam allowance, sew the ruffle's raw ends together. Press the seam open, and topstitch. Baste around the edges of the rectangle.

2. Pin the remaining chintz rectangle to the lace rectangle right sides together, with the ruffle in between. Using a ½-inch seam allowance, stitch around three sides and four corners, leaving a 12-inch opening at the bottom. Trim the seams, but do not turn the quilt right side out yet.

3. Place the batting rectangles underneath the quilt's bottom chintz rectangle. Sew the batting to the quilt along the stitching line, leaving the 12-inch opening at the bottom. Trim the seams, and turn the quilt right side out. Turn in the open edges, and slipstitch the opening closed *(see Stitch Guide, page 168).*

4. Thread the sewing needle with the buttontwist thread. Working from front to back so the knots will be on the front, tack together the quilt front and back at each corner of the lace squares; ribbon bows will cover the thread knots.

5. Cut the ribbon into eight 5-inch lengths, and twenty-four 16-inch lengths. Using the long needle, thread a 16-inch ribbon lengthwise through the lace between two squares *(see photo);* leave about 5 inches of ribbon at each end. Repeat to complete the row. Repeat on the remaining lengthwise rows. There should be two 5-inch-long ribbon ends at each corner of the lace squares; tie the ribbon ends into bows. There should be an extra 5 inches of ribbon at each end of the ribbon rows. Sew one end of a 5-inch ribbon to the quilt where the quilt joins the ruffle at each end of the ribbon rows, and tie a bow. The completed quilt should have 28 bows.

PILLOW

Materials: 1 yard of ivory chintz cotton fabric used in Quilt; ½ yard of lace square fabric used in Quilt; 1½ yards of white ruffled eyelet lace used in Quilt; apricot and white sewing threads; 42 inches of ¼-inch-wide apricot satin ribbon; synthetic stuffing; long needle with large eye.

Directions:

1. Cut the lace fabric into a 12-inch square, or about 2 lace squares by 2 lace squares. Cut two chintz squares to match. Assemble the pillow following Quilt, Steps 1 and 2. Trim the seams, and clip the corners. Turn the pillow right side out, and stuff it. Turn in the open edges, and slipstitch the opening closed.

2. Finish the pillow following Quilt, Step 5; place the ribbons at right angles to each other down the center of the pillow *(see photo).*

PENNSYLVANIA DUTCH CHILD'S ROCKING CHAIR

Average: For those with some experience in woodworking and decorative painting.

Materials: ½-inch-thick birch plywood; 1-inch finishing nails; wood glue; graphite paper; stylus or dry ballpoint pen; fine sandpaper; tack cloth; yellow oxide, chromium green, red, blue and white acrylic paints; paintbrush; artist's paintbrushes; sabre saw, or scroll saw; hammer; tracing paper for patterns.

Directions:

1. Draw the chair back and seat on plywood following the measurements in Fig. V, 13A. Enlarge the chair side pattern in Fig. V, 13B onto tracing paper, following the directions on page 169. Enlarge the patterns for the chair back top and front seat brace designs in Figs. V, 13C and 13D *(pages 146-147)* onto tracing paper, following the directions on page 169. Using the graphite paper and stylus or dry ballpoint pen, transfer the shape of the chair back top to the chair back. Transfer the chair side pattern and the front seat brace shape to the plywood.

2. Cut out the chair pieces. Using glue and nails, assemble the rocking chair following the diagram in Fig. V, 13A. Let the glue dry completely. Sand the chair smooth, and wipe off all the sawdust with the tack cloth.

3. Paint the chair with two coats of yellow oxide, letting the paint dry between coats.

4. Transfer the designs for the chair back and front seat brace to the chair parts. Using the artist's paintbrushes, and the photo as a color guide, paint the designs.

FIG. V, 13A ASSEMBLY DIAGRAM

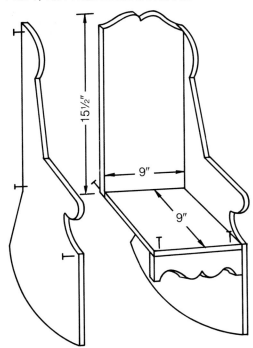

15½"

9"

9"

FIG. V, 13B PENNSYLVANIA DUTCH
CHILD'S ROCKING CHAIR SIDE   1 SQ. = 1"

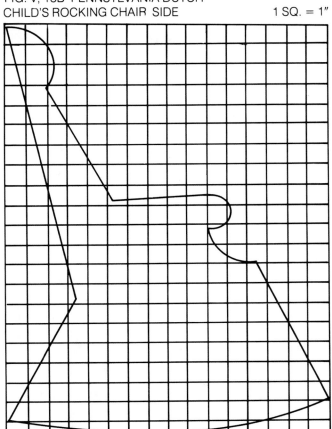

FIG. V, 13D   FRONT SEAT BRACE   1 SQ. = 1"

THE BEAR NECESSITIES

A set of wonderful wooden bear toys to delight both girls and boys.

Average: For those with some experience in woodworking.

TEDDY PULL TOY
(4 x 7½ x 10 inches)

Materials: 12 inches of 1 x 12 pine lumber; ¼-inch-diameter wooden dowel; 1-inch-diameter round wooden knob; four 2-inch-diameter flat wooden knobs; 1 yard of red cord; wood glue; graphite paper; stylus or dry ballpoint pen; sandpaper; tack cloth; red, blue, beige and black acrylic paints; paintbrush; artist's paintbrush; jigsaw, or sabre saw; drill with ¼-inch bit; clamp; tracing paper for pattern.

Cutting Directions

Code	Pieces	Size
A (PINE)	1	¾" x 7" x 9" Bears
B (PINE)	2	¾" x 1¼" x 7½" Frames
C (DOW)	2	¼" dia. x 3¼" Axles
D	4	2" dia. Wheels

Directions:

1. Cut the toy parts to size. Enlarge the bears pattern in Fig. V, 14A onto tracing paper, following the directions on page 169. Using the graphite paper and stylus or dry ballpoint pen, transfer the solid pattern lines to the A bears wood piece. Cut out the bears along the outside line. Cut the inside line that separates the parent from the baby bear.

2. Drill a ¼-inch-diameter hole, centered, ⅝ inch in from each end of the B frames. Drill a ¼-inch-diameter hole in each D flat knob wheel to accommodate the C axles, and in the round knob to accommodate the cord *(see Fig. V, 14B, page 150)*.

3. Sand all the wood pieces smooth, sanding the A bears' inside edges lightly for a snug fit. Wipe off all the sawdust with the tack cloth.

(Continued on page 150)

FIG. V, 14A   TEDDY PULL TOY

1 SQ. = 1″

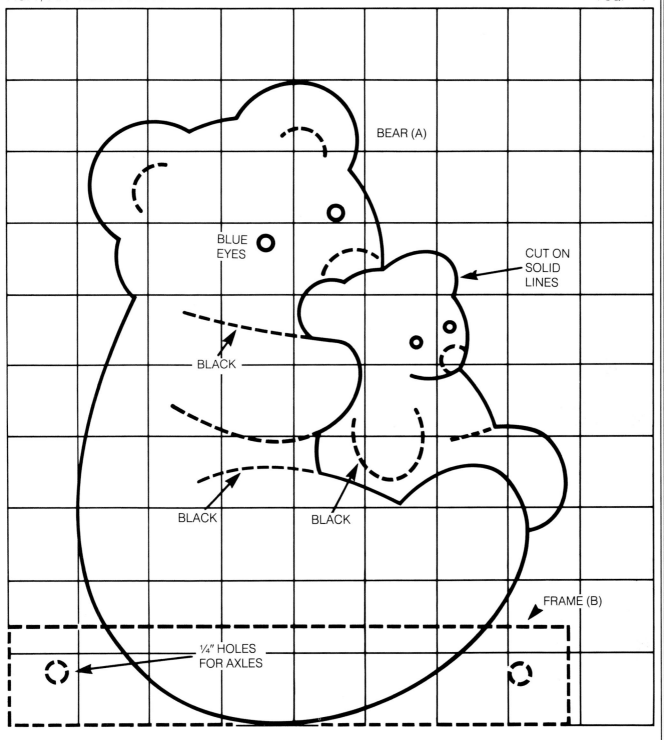

BEAR (A)

BLUE
EYES

CUT ON
SOLID
LINES

BLACK

BLACK

BLACK

FRAME (B)

¼″ HOLES
FOR AXLES

4. Paint the A bears beige. Paint the B frames red. Paint the D flat knob wheels and the round knob blue. Transfer the bear features to both sides of the A bears. Using the artist's paintbrush, and following FIG. V, 14A *(page 149)*, paint the bear features.

5. Place the C axles in the holes of the B frames. Glue the A bears between the B frames centered lengthwise, and flush at the bottom *(see* FIG. V, 14A*)*. Clamp all the pieces to hold them in place, making sure the C axles are straight and square. Let the glue dry completely.

6. Glue a D flat knob wheel on each end of the C axles. Feed one end of the cord into the hole in the round knob, and glue the end in place. Tie the other end of the cord around the front C axle.

FIG. V, 14B   ASSEMBLY DIAGRAM

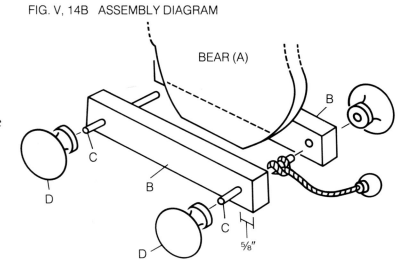

BEAR (A)

FIG. V, 14C   BABY BEAR PUZZLE   FULL SIZE

BEAR FAMILY PUZZLES

Materials: ¾ x 10 x 24 inches of birch plywood; wood glue; graphite paper; stylus or dry ballpoint pen; sandpaper; tack cloth; butcher's wax; clean cloth; jigsaw, or sabre saw; drill with ¼-inch bit; tracing paper.

Directions:

1. Cut the plywood into four 5 x 7½-inch pieces, and two 4 x 5-inch pieces. Glue together pairs of the same size pieces to form two pieces measuring 1½ x 5 x 7½ inches, and one piece measuring 1½ x 4 x 5 inches.

2. Trace the full-size baby bear pattern in FIG. V, 14C onto tracing paper. Trace the full-size mama bear and papa bear half patterns in FIG. V, 14D onto folded sheets of tracing paper. Trace the patterns onto the other halves of the papers, and open the papers for the full patterns. Using the graphite paper and stylus or dry ballpoint pen, transfer all the patterns to the plywood.

3. Cut out the bear shapes. Cut the puzzle lines. Cut out the papa bear's bow tie by drilling through the center of the tie, putting the saw blade in the hole, and cutting. Drill the eye holes to the depth of the bit angle.

4. Sand the puzzle pieces smooth, and wipe off all the sawdust with the tack cloth. Coat the puzzle pieces with the butcher's wax.

FIG. V, 14D   MAMA & PAPA BEAR PUZZLES   FULL SIZE

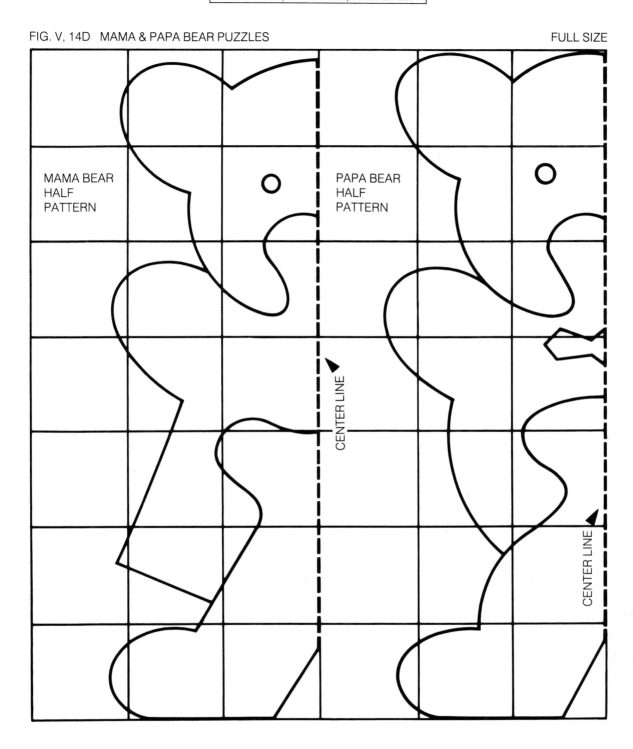

MAMA BEAR
HALF
PATTERN

PAPA BEAR
HALF
PATTERN

CENTER LINE

CENTER LINE

Pooling Your Resources

During the Christmas shopping season, you and every one of your friends are bound to make one trip to the mall. Why not join forces and car pool?

Car pooling is a wonderful idea any time of year, but especially during the busy holiday season. By taking one car at a time, you'll all save on fuel. Plus, you'll have an easier time parking one car in the crowded mall parking lot.

Try organizing a neighborhood "pooling" system to take some of the bother out of holiday trips to the mall, post office, supermarket, and even to pick up the kids at school.

BEAR CLOTHES RACK

Materials: 14 inches of 1 x 10 pine lumber; two 2-inch-diameter wooden door pulls; graphite paper; stylus or dry ballpoint pen; sandpaper; tack cloth; red, blue, yellow, green, beige and black acrylic paints; paintbrush; artist's paintbrushes; jigsaw, or sabre saw; drill with small bit; 2 sawtooth hangers; paper for pattern.

Directions:

1. Enlarge the bears pattern in FIG. V, 14E onto paper, following the directions on page 169. Using the graphite paper and stylus or dry ballpoint pen, transfer the solid pattern line to the pine. Cut out the bears. Do not cut between the bears; the rack is one piece joined at the bears' feet.

2. Sand the rack and door pulls smooth, and wipe off all the sawdust with the tack cloth.

3. Paint the rack beige. Transfer the bear features to the rack, and the ball designs to the door pulls. Using the artist's paintbrushes, and following FIG. V, 14E, paint the bear features and ball designs. Let dry completely.

4. Drill shallow starter holes in the rack where indicated in FIG. V, 14E for the door pulls. Screw the door pulls in place.

5. Attach a sawtooth hanger to the back of each bear's head, making sure the hangers are level.

OB = OVERALL BEIGE
G = GREEN
R = RED
BL = BLACK
Y = YELLOW
B = BLUE

FIG. V, 14E BEAR CLOTHES RACK

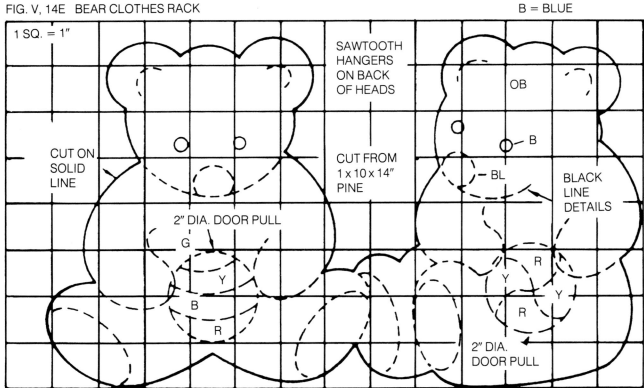

152

PULL-ALONG DINOSAUR

Average: For those with some experience in woodworking.

Materials: 3 feet of 6-inch-wide, ½-inch-thick clear pine or hardwood; ¼-inch- and 1½-inch-diameter wooden dowels; large wooden bead; two 72-inch-long rawhide shoestrings; white glue; graphite paper; stylus or dry ballpoint pen; sandpaper; tack cloth; jigsaw, or coping saw; drill with assorted bits; paper for pattern.

Directions:
1. Enlarge the dinosaur pattern in FIG. V, 15 *(page 154)* onto paper, following the directions on page 169. Using the graphite paper and stylus or dry ballpoint pen, transfer the pattern

pieces to the pine or hardwood, laying the pieces so the wood grain runs up and down the dinosaur body. Transfer two hind legs, two front legs, and one each of the body pieces.
2. Cut out the dinosaur parts. From the 1½-inch-diameter dowel, cut four ½-inch-thick circles for wheels. From the ¼-inch-diameter dowel, cut two 4-inch lengths for axles, and two 2½-inch lengths for pegs.
3. Drill ⁵⁄₁₆-inch-diameter holes through the feet on the front and hind legs so the axles will revolve freely. Drill ¼-inch-diameter holes through the tops of the front and hind legs, and through the body pieces where the legs will be attached *(see circles on pattern in* FIG. V, 15*)*. Drill ¼-inch-diameter holes through the centers of the wheels. Drill small holes, just enough for the rawhide shoestring

to slip through easily, where the body pieces will be connected, and at the dinosaur's mouth and eye *(see dots on pattern in* FIG. V, 15*)*. Sand the pieces smooth, and wipe off all the sawdust with the tack cloth.
4. Using one rawhide shoestring, cut and thread a length of rawhide through each small hole where the body pieces will be connected. Tie the body pieces together with the rawhide, tying each pair of lengths into a square knot on each side of the body. Trim the rawhide ends, and place a dot of glue on each end to prevent the rawhide from untying.
5. Place generous amounts of glue around the ¼-inch-diameter body and leg holes. Slip the pegs into the body holes, and attach the legs to the ends of the pegs, making sure the peg ends are flush with the legs' outside

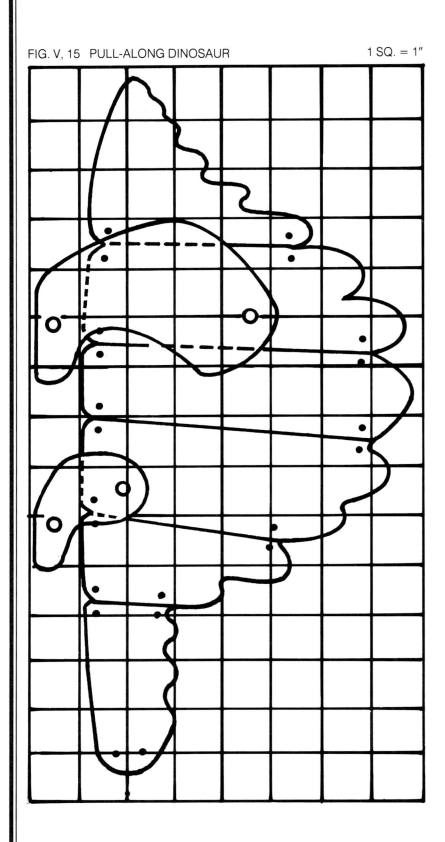

edges. Slip the axles through the holes in the feet, and glue a wheel flush on each end. Before the glue dries, angle the legs properly so all the wheels touch the ground. Let the glue dry completely.

6. Sand the ends of the pegs and axles. Thread and tie one end of the remaining rawhide shoestring through the hole at the dinosaur's mouth. Tie the wooden bead to the other end of the shoestring for a pull.

SIT-ON LOCOMOTIVE
(8 x 11 x 22 inches)

Challenging: Requires more experience in woodworking.

Materials: 48 inches of ⁵⁄₄ x 6 pine lumber; 5 feet of 1 x 8 pine lumber; 7 feet of ¼ x 1-inch, and 12 feet of ¼ x ⅝-inch lattice; 1¼-inch-diameter clothes pole dowel; 1-inch-, ⅞-inch-, ½-inch- and ⅜-inch-diameter wooden dowels; 3½-inch-long common nail; ¾-inch wire brads; 4d and 6d finishing nails; four ¾-inch No. 10 panhead sheet metal screws; two ¾-inch No. 8 panhead sheet metal screws; four ¾-inch No. 6 panhead sheet metal screws; two 1½-inch No. 8 flathead wood screws; three 1¼-inch No. 8 flathead wood screws; two ⅞-inch I.D. washers; ten ½-inch I.D. washers; four ¾-inch O.D. washers; six ⅜-inch O.D. washers; 1½-inch-long, 1-inch-diameter brass bell; wood glue; graphite paper; stylus or dry ballpoint pen; sandpaper; tack cloth; red, green, light blue, royal blue, silver and black glossy paints, or colors desired; clear gloss polyurethane; paintbrushes; saw; backsaw; miter box; drill with assorted bits; screwdriver; hammer; paper for pattern.

Directions:

1. Trace the full-size cab patterns in FIGS. V, 16B and 16C onto paper. Using the graphite paper and stylus or

dry ballpoint pen, transfer the pattern pieces to 1 x 8 pine. Cut out the D cab front, D1 cab sides, and D2 cab back.

2. Refer to the Cutting Directions to cut the C engine ribs, J cowcatcher and A engine bottom pieces. Shape them following the measurements in FIG. V, 16A. Cut the other locomotive parts to size.

3. Sand the locomotive parts smooth, and wipe off all the sawdust with the tack cloth. Following the diagrams in FIG. V, 16D, and using glue and nails or screws, assemble the cab, engine, chimney/handle, and cowcatcher.

4. Using the photo as a color guide, paint the cab, engine, pistons, chimney/handle, cowcatcher, wheels and wheel shafts. Apply a coat of polyurethane to the seat. Let the paint and polyurethane dry completely.

5. Finish assembling the locomotive. Shape the common nail into the K bell support, slide the bell onto it, and attach it to the C3 engine front *(see photo and* FIG. V, 16D*).*

Cutting Directions

Code	Pieces	Size
A (PINE)	1	1¼″ x 2½″ x 20″ Engine bottom
B (PINE)	2	¾″ x 3⅝″ x 17″ Engine sides
C (PINE)	3	¾″ x 3½″ x 5¼″ Engine ribs
C1 (PINE)	1	1¼″ x 1½″ x 3½″ Handle support
C2 (PINE)	1	¾″ x 2½″ x 2½″ Engine rib
C3 (PINE)	1	1¼″ x 4″ dia. Engine front
C4 (LAT)	2	¼″ x ⅞″ x 11¾″ Engine rails
C5 (LAT)	8	¼″ x ⅝″ x 11¾″ Engine top
D (PINE)	1	¾″ x 5″ x 7″ Cab front
D1 (PINE)	2	¾″ x 4″ x 6″ Cab sides
D2 (PINE)	1	¾″ x 2″ x 6½″ Cab back
D3 (LAT)	8	¼″ x 1″ x 6¼″ Cab roof

Code	Pieces	Size
E (PINE)	1	¾″ x 5½″ x 5¾″ Seat
F (DOW)	2	1¼″ dia. x 4″ Pistons
G (DOW)	4	½″ dia. x 3″ Axles
G1 (PINE)	4	1¼″ x 5¼″ dia. Wheels
G2 (DOW)	4	⅜″ dia. x ⅜″ Spacers
G3 (LAT)	2	¼″ x ⅝″ x 7″ Wheel shafts
H (DOW)	1	1¼″ dia. x 4″ Front axle support
H1 (DOW)	2	⅜″ dia. x 3″ Front axles
H2 (DOW)	1	⅞″ dia. x 11″ Chimney
H3 (DOW)	1	1″ dia. x 4½″ Handle
H4 (PINE)	2	¾″ x 1¾″ dia. Wheels
J (PINE)	2	¾″ x 3½″ x 5½″ Cowcatcher
K	1	3½″ Bell support

FIG. V, 16A SIT-ON LOCOMOTIVE CUTTING DIAGRAMS

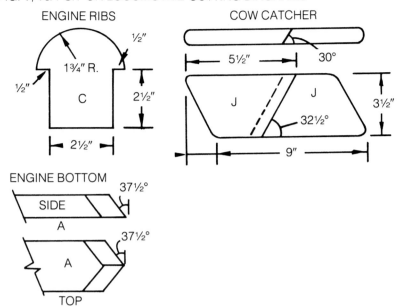

ENGINE RIBS

1¾" R.

½"

½"

C

2½"

2½"

COW CATCHER

5½"

30°

J

J

3½"

32½°

9"

ENGINE BOTTOM

37½°

SIDE

A

37½°

A

TOP

FIG. V, 16B CAB FRONT AND BACK

FULL SIZE

D2

D

FIG. V, 16D   ASSEMBLY DIAGRAMS

FRONT VIEW

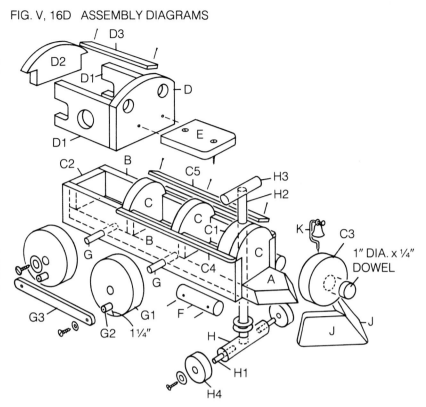

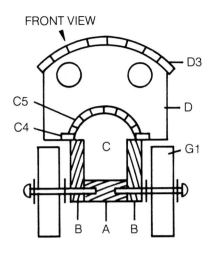

ENGINE SIDES (B)

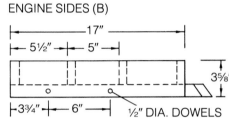

17"

5½"   5"

3⅝"

3¾"   6"   ½" DIA. DOWELS

FIG. V, 16C   CAB SIDE   FULL SIZE

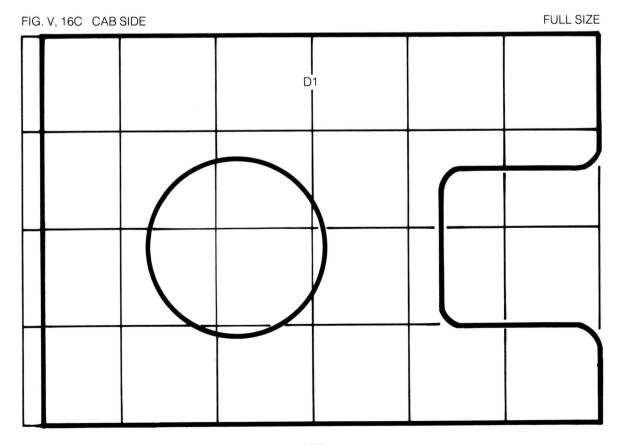

D1

CRAFTS BASICS & ABBREVIATIONS

HOW TO KNIT

THE BASIC STITCHES

Get out your needles and yarn, and slowly read your way through this special section. Practice the basic stitches illustrated here as you go along. Once you know them, you're ready to start knitting.

CASTING ON: This puts the first row of stitches on the needle. Measure off about two yards of yarn (or about an inch for each stitch you are going to cast on). Make a slip knot at this point by making a medium-size loop of yarn; then pull another small loop through it. Place the slip knot on one needle and pull one end gently to tighten (FIG. 1).

FIG. 1

• Hold the needle in your right hand. Hold both strands of yarn in the palm of your left hand securely but not rigidly. Slide your left thumb and forefinger between the two strands and spread these two fingers out so that you have formed a triangle of yarn.
• Your left thumb should hold the free end of yarn, your forefinger the yarn from the ball. The needle in your right hand holds the first stitch (FIG. 2).

FIG. 2

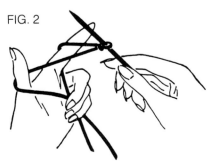

You are now in position to cast on.
• Bring the needle in your right hand toward you; slip the tip of the needle under the front strand of the loop on your left thumb (FIG. 3).

FIG. 3

• Now, with the needle, catch the strand of yarn that is on your left forefinger (FIG. 4).

FIG. 4

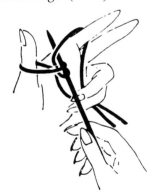

• Draw it through the thumb loop to form a stitch on the needle (FIG. 5).

FIG. 5

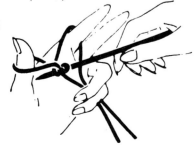

KNITTING ABBREVIATIONS AND SYMBOLS

Knitting directions are always written in standard abbreviations. Although they may look confusing, with practice you'll soon know them:

beg—beginning; **bet**—between; **bl**—block; **ch**—chain; **CC**—contrasting color; **dec(s)**—decrease(s); **dp**—double-pointed; " or **in(s)**—inch(es); **incl**—inclusive; **inc(s)**—increase(s); **k**—knit; **lp(s)**—loop(s); **MC**—main color; **oz(s)**—ounces(s); **psso**—pass slipped stitch over last stitch worked; **pat(s)**—pattern(s); **p**—purl; **rem**—remaining; **rpt**—repeat; **rnd(s)**—round(s); **sk**—skip; **sl**—slip; **sl st**—slip stitch; **sp(s),**—space(s); **st(s)**—stitch(es); **st st**—stockinette stitch; **tog**—together, **yo**—yarn over; **pc**—popcorn stitch.

* (asterisk)—directions immediately following * are to be repeated the specified number of times indicated in addition to the first time—i.e. "repeat from * 3 times more" means 4 times in all.

( ) (parentheses)—directions should be worked as often as specified—i.e., "(k 1, k 2 tog, k 3) 5 times" means to work what is in ( ) 5 times in all.

• Holding the stitch on the needle with your right index finger, slip the loop off your left thumb (FIG. 6). Tighten up the stitch on the needle by pulling the freed strand back with your left thumb, bringing the yarn back into position for casting on more stitches (FIG. 2).

FIG. 6

• **Do not cast on too tightly.** Stitches should slide easily on the needle. Repeat from * until you have cast on the number of stitches specified in your instructions.

KNIT STITCH (k): Hold the needle with the cast-on stitches in your left hand (FIG. 7).

FIG. 7

• Pick up the other needle in your right hand. With yarn from the ball in **back** (the side farthest away from you) of the work, insert the tip of the right-hand needle from **left to right** through the front loop of the first stitch on the left-hand needle (FIG. 8).

FIG. 8

• Holding both needles in this position with your left hand, wrap the yarn over your little finger, under your two middle fingers and over the forefinger of your right hand. Hold the yarn firmly, but loosely enough so that it will slide through your fingers as you knit. Return the right-hand needle to your right hand.

• With your right forefinger, pass the yarn under (from right to left) and then over (from left to right) the tip of the right-hand needle, forming a loop on the needle (FIG. 9).

FIG. 9

• Now draw this loop through the stitch on the left-hand needle (FIG. 10).

FIG. 10

• Slip the original stitch off the left-hand needle, leaving the new stitch on right-hand needle (FIG. 11).

FIG. 11

Note: *Keep the stitches loose enough to slide along the needles, but tight enough to maintain their position on the needles until you want them to slide.* Continue until you have knitted all the stitches from the left-hand needle onto the right-hand needle.

• To start the next row, pass the needle with stitches on it to your left hand, reversing it, so that it is now the left-hand needle.

PURL STITCH (p): Purling is the reverse of knitting. Again, keep the stitches loose enough to slide, but firm enough to work with. To purl, hold the needle with the stitches in your left hand, with the yarn in *front* of your work. Insert the tip of the right-hand needle from *right to left* through the front loop of the first stitch on the left-hand needle (FIG. 12).

FIG. 12

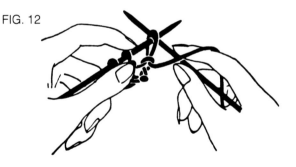

• With your right hand holding the yarn as you would to knit, but in *front* of the needles, pass the yarn over the tip of the right-hand needle, then under it, forming a loop on the needle (FIG. 13).

FIG. 13

• Holding the yarn firmly so that it won't slip off, draw this loop through the stitch on the left-hand needle (FIG. 14).

FIG. 14

• Slip the original stitch off of the left-hand needle, leaving the new stitch on the right-hand needle (FIG. 15).

FIG. 15

SLIPSTITCH (sl st): Insert the tip of the right-hand needle into the next stitch on the left-hand needle, as if to purl, unless otherwise directed. Slip this stitch off the left-hand needle onto the right, but *do not* work the stitch (FIG. 16).

FIG. 16

3. _To increase by "yarn-over" (yo):_ Pass the yarn **over** the right-hand needle after finishing one stitch and before starting the next stitch, making an extra stitch (see the arrow in FIG. 23). If you are knitting, bring the yarn **under** the needle to the back. If you are purling, wind the yarn **around** the needle once. On the next row, work all yarn-overs as stitches.

FIG. 23

DECREASING (dec): This means reducing the number of stitches in a given area to shape your work. Two methods for decreasing are:

1. _To decrease by knitting_ (FIG. 24) _or purling_ (FIG. 25) _two stitches together:_

FIG. 24

FIG. 25

Insert the right-hand needle through the loops of two stitches on the left-hand needle at the same time. Complete the stitch. This is written as "k 2 tog" or "p 2 tog."

• If you work through the **front** loops of the stitches, your decreasing stitch will slant to the right. If you work through the **back** loops of the stitches, your decreasing stitch will slant to the left.

2. _Slip 1 stitch, knit 1 and psso:_ Insert the right-hand needle through the stitch on the left-hand needle, but instead of working it, just slip it off onto the right-hand needle (see FIG. 16). Work the next stitch in the usual way. With the tip of the left-hand needle, lift the slipped stitch over the last stitch worked and off the tip of the right-hand needle (FIG. 26).
Your decreasing stitch will slant to the left. This is written as "sl 1, k 1, psso."

FIG. 26

Pass Slipped Stitch Over (psso): Slip one stitch from the left-hand needle to the right-hand needle and, being careful to keep it in position, work the next stitch. Then, with the tip of the left-hand needle, lift the slipped stitch over the last stitch and off the tip of the right-hand needle (FIG. 26).

ATTACHING YARN

When you finish one ball of yarn, or if you wish to change colors, attach the new ball of yarn at the start of a row. Tie the new yarn to an end of the previous yarn, making a secure knot to join the two yarns. Continue to work (FIG. 27).

FIG. 27

HOW TO CROCHET

THE BASIC STITCHES

Most crochet stitches are started from a base of chain stitches. However, our stitches are started from a row of single crochet stitches which gives body to the sample swatches and makes practice work easier to handle. When making a specific item, follow the stitch directions as given.

• Holding the crochet hook properly (FIG. 1), start by practicing the slip knot (FIG. 2A through FIG. 2D) and base chain (FIG. 3A through FIG. 3C).

CHAIN STITCH (cb): Follow the steps in FIG. 3A through FIG. 3C. As you make the chain stitch loops, the yarn should slide easily between your index and middle fingers. Make about 15 loops. If they are all the same size, you have maintained even tension. If the stitches are uneven, rip them out by pulling on the long end of the yarn. Practice the chain stitch until you can crochet a perfect chain.

From here on, we won't be showing hands—just the hook and the stitches. ***Note:*** *Left-handed crocheters can use the illustrations for right-handed crocheting by turning the book upside down in front of a free-standing mirror. The reflected illustrations will provide left-handed instructions.*

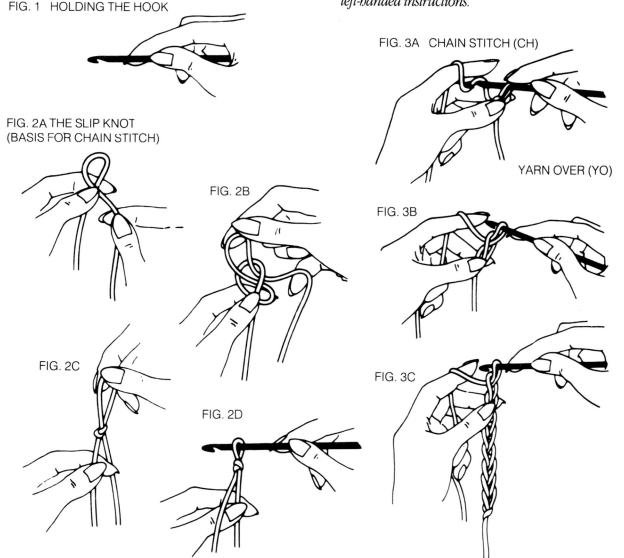

FIG. 1   HOLDING THE HOOK

FIG. 2A THE SLIP KNOT
(BASIS FOR CHAIN STITCH)

FIG. 2B

FIG. 2C

FIG. 2D

FIG. 3A   CHAIN STITCH (CH)

YARN OVER (YO)

FIG. 3B

FIG. 3C

CROCHET ABBREVIATIONS AND SYMBOLS

The following is a list of standard crochet abbreviations with definitions of the terms given. To help you become accustomed to the abbreviations used, we have repeated them throughout our instructions.

beg — begin, beginning; **ch** — chain; **dc** — double crochet; **dec** — decrease; **dtr** — double treble crochet; **hdc** — half double crochet; **in(s)** or **″** — inch(es); **inc** — increase; **oz(s)** — ounce(s); **pat** — pattern; **pc** — picot; **rem** — remaining; **rnd** — round; **rpt** — repeat; **sc** — single crochet; **skn(s)** — skein(s); **sk** — skip; **sl st** — slip stitch; **sp** — space; **st(s)** — stitch(es); **tog** — together; **tr** — triple crochet; **work even** — continue without further increase or decrease; **yo** — yarn over.

* (asterisk) — directions immediately following * are to be repeated the specified number of times indicated in addition to the first time.

( ) (parentheses) — directions should be worked as often as specified.

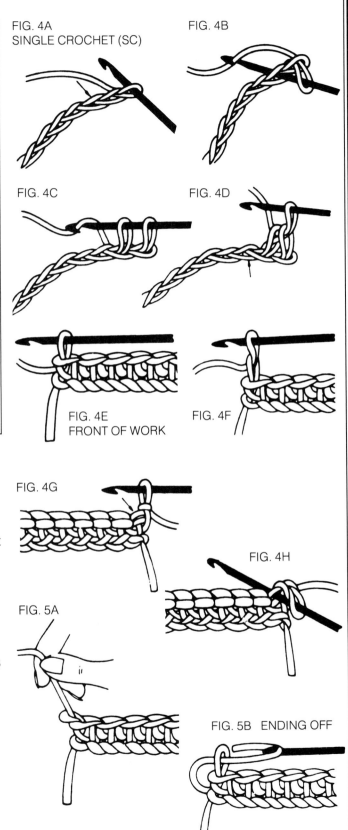

FIG. 4A
SINGLE CROCHET (SC)

FIG. 4B

FIG. 4C

FIG. 4D

FIG. 4E
FRONT OF WORK

FIG. 4F

FIG. 4G

FIG. 4H

FIG. 5A

FIG. 5B ENDING OFF

SINGLE CROCHET (sc): Follow the steps in (FIG. 4A through FIG. 4H). To practice, make a 20-loop chain (this means 20 loops in addition to the slip knot). Turn the chain, as shown, and insert the hook in the second chain from the hook (see arrow) to make the first sc stitch. Yarn over (yo); for the second stitch, see the next arrow. Repeat to the end of the chain. Because you started in the second chain from the hook, you end up with only 19 sc. To add the 20th stitch, ch 1 (called a turning chain) and pull the yarn through. Now turn your work around (the "back" is now facing you) and start the second row of sc in the first stitch of the previous row (at the arrow). Make sure your hook goes under both of the strands at the top of the stitch. Don't forget to make a ch 1 turning chain at the end before turning your work. Keep practicing until your rows are perfect.

ENDING OFF: Follow the steps in (FIG. 5A and FIG. 5B). To finish off your crochet, cut off all but 6-inches of yarn and end off as shown. (To "break off and fasten," follow the same procedure.)

DOUBLE CROCHET (dc): Follow the steps in (Fig. 6A through Fig. 6F). To practice, ch 20, then make a row of 20 sc. Now, instead of a ch 1, you will make a ch 3. Turn your work, yo and insert the hook in the second stitch of the previous row (at the arrow), going under both strands at the top of the stitch. Pull the yarn through. You now have three loops on the hook. Yo and pull through the first two, then yo and pull through the remaining two—one double crochet (dc) made. Continue across the row, making a dc in each stitch (st) across. Dc in the top of the turning chain (see arrow in Fig. 7). Ch 3. Turn work. Dc in second stitch on the previous row and continue as before.

FIG. 7

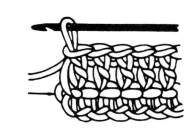

Note: *You may also start a row of dc on a base chain (omitting the sc row). In this case, insert the hook in the fourth chain from the hook, instead of the second (Fig. 8).*

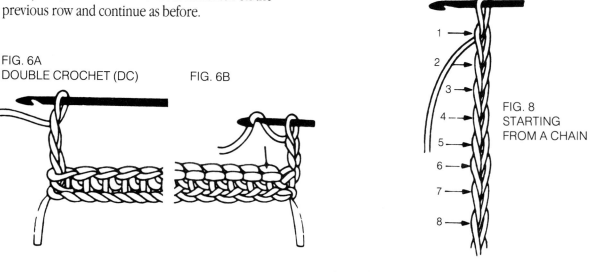

FIG. 8
STARTING
FROM A CHAIN

FIG. 6A
DOUBLE CROCHET (DC)   FIG. 6B

FIG. 6C   FIG. 6D

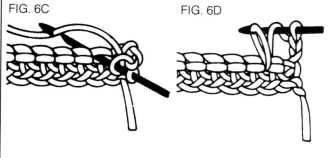

SLIP STITCH (sl st): Follow the steps in Fig. 9A. This is the stitch you will use for joining, shaping and ending off. After you chain and turn, *do not* yo. Just insert the hook into the *first* stitch of the previous row (see Fig. 9A and Fig. 9B), and pull the yarn through the stitch, then through the loop on the hook—the sl st is made.

FIG. 6E   FIG. 6F

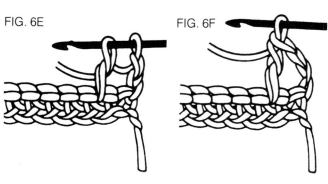

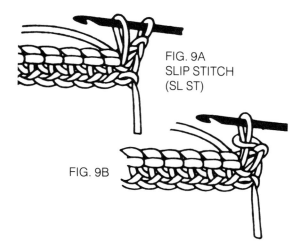

FIG. 9A
SLIP STITCH
(SL ST)

FIG. 9B

DOUBLE CROCHET (dc): Follow the steps in (FIG. 6A through FIG. 6F). To practice, ch 20, then make a row of 20 sc. Now, instead of a ch 1, you will make a ch 3. Turn your work, yo and insert the hook in the second stitch of the previous row (at the arrow), going under both strands at the top of the stitch. Pull the yarn through. You now have three loops on the hook. Yo and pull through the first two, then yo and pull through the remaining two—one double crochet (dc) made. Continue across the row, making a dc in each stitch (st) across. Dc in the top of the turning chain (see arrow in FIG. 7). Ch 3. Turn work. Dc in second stitch on the previous row and continue as before.

FIG. 7

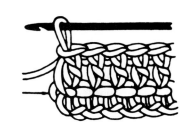

Note: *You may also start a row of dc on a base chain (omitting the sc row). In this case, insert the hook in the fourth chain from the hook, instead of the second (FIG. 8).*

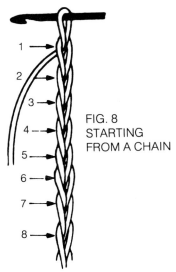

FIG. 8
STARTING
FROM A CHAIN

FIG. 6A
DOUBLE CROCHET (DC)   FIG. 6B

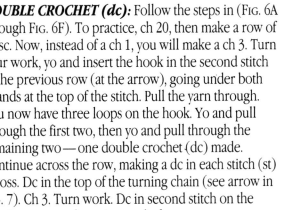

FIG. 6C   FIG. 6D

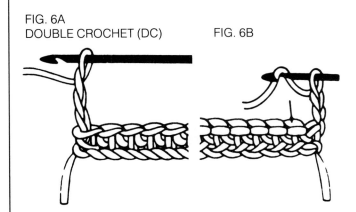

FIG. 6E   FIG. 6F

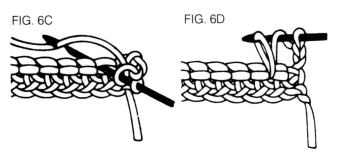

SLIP STITCH (sl st): Follow the steps in FIG. 9A. This is the stitch you will use for joining, shaping and ending off. After you chain and turn, ***do not*** yo. Just insert the hook into the ***first*** stitch of the previous row (see FIG. 9A and FIG. 9B), and pull the yarn through the stitch, then through the loop on the hook—the sl st is made.

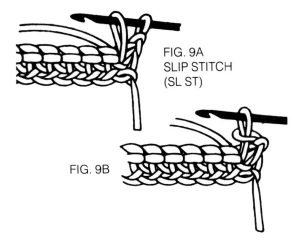

FIG. 9A
SLIP STITCH
(SL ST)

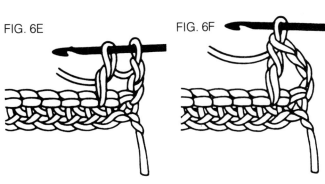

FIG. 9B

HALF DOUBLE CROCHET (hdc): Follow the steps in Figs. 10A and 10B.

To practice, make a chain and a row of sc. Ch 2 and turn; yo. Insert the hook in the second stitch, as shown; yo and pull through to make three loops on the hook. Yo and pull the yarn through *all* three loops at the same time—hdc made. This stitch primarily is used as a transitional stitch from an sc to a dc. Try it and see—starting with sc's, then an hdc and then dc's.

FIG. 10A
HALF DOUBLE CROCHET

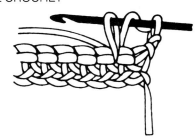

FIG. 10B

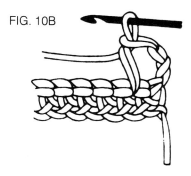

SHAPING TECHNIQUES FOR CROCHETING

Now that you have practiced and made sample squares of all the basic stitches, you are ready to learn the adding and subtracting stitches that will shape your project by changing the length of a row as per the instructions. This is done by increasing (inc) and decreasing (dec).

To increase (inc): Just make two stitches in the same stitch in the previous row (see arrow in Fig. 11). The technique is the same for any kind of stitch.

FIG. 11   INCREASING (INC)
FOR SINGLE CROCHET

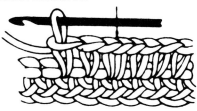

To decrease (dec) for single-crochet (sc): Yo and pull the yarn through two stitches to make three loops on the hook (see steps in Figs. 12A and 12B). Pull the yarn through all the loops at once—dec made. Continue in the stitches called for in the instructions.

FIG. 12A   DECREASING (DEC)

FOR SINGLE CROCHET   FIG. 12B

To decrease for double crochet (dc): In a dc row, make the next stitch and stop when you have two loops on the hook. Now yo and make a dc in the next stitch. At the point where you have three loops on the hook, pull yarn through all loops at the same time. Finish the row with regular dc.

HOW TO BLOCK LIKE A PRO

These step-by-step instructions for blocking will insure that your needlework has a professional finished look.

MATERIALS:

• *A Blocking Board* An absolute *must* for professional-looking blocking. You can usually buy a blocking board at craft and sewing centers.
• *Rustproof T-pins and Staples* Used to hold the needlework pieces in place.
• *Undyed Cotton Cloth* A dampened cloth covers the needlework while it is being pressed.
• *Iron* With a dry setting.
• *Yellow Soap* Dels Naptha or Kirkman. For blocking needlepoint. Restores natural sizing to canvas and helps prevent infestations of insects.

KNITTED OR CROCHETED WORK:

The purpose of blocking is to align the stitches, loft the yarn and straighten the knitted or crocheted pieces.
• Pin the work or the pieces, right side down, to the blocking board with the T-pins. Place the pins close together to avoid ripples in the work.
• Dampen a cotton cloth with water and wring it out; the cloth should be moist, not dripping wet. Place the cloth over the work on the board.
• Set the iron on "dry" and select a temperature setting suited to the fibers in the work.
• Gently iron over the cloth in the direction of the stitches. *Do not* apply pressure to the iron or iron against the grain. You may need to remoisten the cloth and iron the work several times, until it is moist and warm to the touch.
• Carefully remove the cloth. If the cloth clings, leaving the work damp and rippled, don't panic. This occurs when a synthetic fiber is pressed with steam that is too hot. No permanent damage can be done unless pressure is used and the stitches are flattened. To restore the work to the desired shape, pat the pieces gently with your hands.
• Allow the work to dry on the board in a flat position for at least 24 hours.
• When the work is completely dry, remove the pins; the pieces are ready to be assembled.

Note: You can ease or stretch pieces a bit to achieve the desired size, but you can't turn a size 10 sweater into a size 16, or shrink a size 40 vest into a size 34.

NEEDLEPOINT PROJECTS:

Blocking needlepoint realigns the threads of the canvas, lofts the yarn and naturally sets each stitch.
*Note: Check for yarn color fastness before you begin to needlepoint. If you've completed a work, and are unsure of the color fastness, **do not block.** Press the work on the wrong side with a warm iron. This won't yield the same results, but avoids color streaking.*
• Place a bar of yellow soap in a bowl of warm water; let it stand until the water is slick to the touch.
• Place the work, right side down, on the blocking board.
• Dip a cotton cloth into the soapy water and wring it out. Place the damp cloth over the needlepoint.
• Set an iron on "dry" with temperature suited to fibers in the work. Lightly iron the cloth; *do not* apply pressure.
• Repeat dampening the cloth and pressing until the canvas is very soft and flexible; moist, but not wet.
• Turn the needlepoint right side up on the board.
• Keeping the threads of the canvas parallel to the grid on the blocking board, staple the canvas to the board leaving 1 inch between the staples and the edge of the needlepoint. (Remove tape or selvages before stapling.) The staples should be fairly close together (do not use pins; staples maintain a straight line and even tension across the work).
• Staple along the bottom edge of the canvas, again, maintaining an even tension across the work. Gently pull one side of the canvas to align the fabric grain with the grid lines on the board, and staple along this edge. Repeat on the other side of the canvas. (*Do not* stretch the canvas; just pull it gently into its original size.) As you are aligning the third and fourth sides, wrinkles may appear in the center of the work; as the fourth side is eased into alignment, these should disappear. If the canvas is pulled off the grain while being blocked, remove the staples and realign the sides. When the grain of the work is perfectly square, the stitching should be aligned; you are not straightening the stitching, you are squaring the threads of the canvas.
• Allow the needlepoint to dry for at least 24 hours.
• When the needlepoint is completely dry, gently pull it up from the board; the staples will pull out easily. Your needlepoint is now ready to be finished.

Note: If the design becomes distorted, reblock the piece.

STITCH GUIDE

BLIND STITCH

SLIP STITCH

BLANKET STITCH

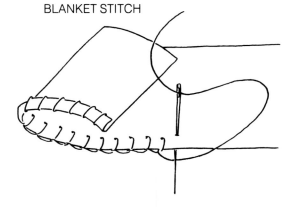

FRENCH KNOT

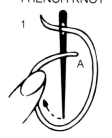
1

2

3

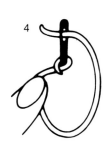
4

SATIN STITCH

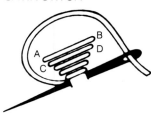

SPLIT STITCH

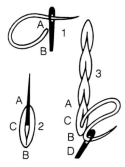

CONTINENTAL STITCH

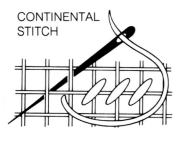

STEM STITCH

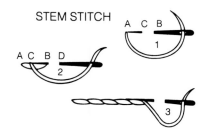

STRAIGHT STITCH

CROSS STITCH

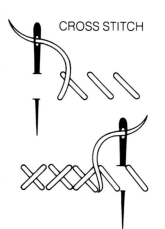

WHIPSTITCH

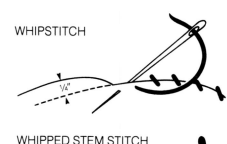

WHIPPED STEM STITCH

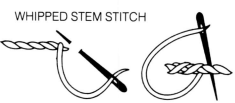

168

CHAIN STITCH

LAZY DAISY STITCH

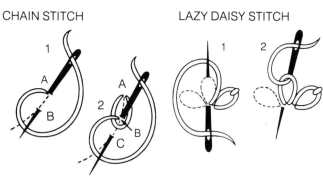

HOW TO ENLARGE PATTERNS AND DESIGNS

If the pattern or design is not already marked off in squares, make a tracing of it. Mark the tracing off in squares: For a small design, make the squares ¼-inch; for larger designs, use ½- or 2-inch squares, or use the size indicated in the directions. Check the instructions for desired size of the finished project. On a second piece of tracing paper, mark off an enlarged grid with the same number of squares as appears on the original pattern. For example, if you wish the finished project to be 6 times larger than the original pattern, each new square must be 6 times larger than on the original. Copy the design outline from the original pattern or tracing onto the second, enlarged grid, square by square. Using a dressmaker's carbon and a tracing wheel, transfer the enlarged design onto the material you are using for your project.

LONG AND SHORT STITCH

BACKSTITCH

CRETAN STITCH

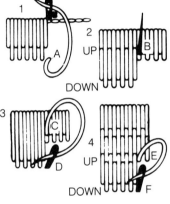

SCOTCH STITCH

BARGELLO STITCH

MESHES

COUCH STITCH

DUPLICATE STITCH

BULLION STITCH

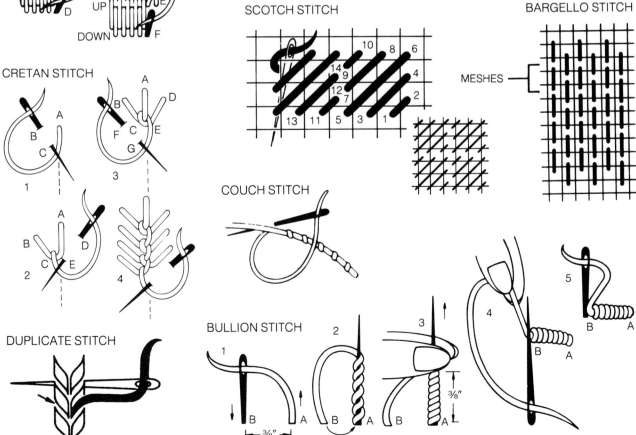

INDEX

A

afghan, Pineapple, *106*-107
angel
    Golden, *32*-34
    Herald, Tree Topper, *86*-87
Antique Doll Wreath, *3*-6
appliqué, Cookie Cutter, *91*
aran, Woman's Knit Sweater, *114*-116

B

baby, Buttercup, Set, *141*, 140-143
bag, Lacy Crochet Tote, *120*-121
basket
    A Symphony in Silver, *94*
    Poinsettia, *21, 28*-29
bear
    Clothes Rack, *148*, 152
    Family Puzzles, *148*, 150-151
    Holly, Wreath, *12*-13
    Teddy-, Pull Toy, *148*-150
    The, Necessities, *148*-152
bell, Wooden, Ornament, *80*
birch, Rustic, Candleholders, *95*
birds, Wooden, Ornament, 80, *82*
book, Take a Note!, *89, 102*
bowl, A Pretty, of Posies, *51*
bow, Crepe Paper Flowers with, *48*-49
box, Mountain Scene Marquetry, *122*-125
Breakfast in Bed Tray & Napkin Rings, *98*-99
Buttercup Baby Set, *141*, 140-143
By Candlelight, *94*

C

candle, 23, 95
    By Candlelight, *94*
    Christmas Kitchen Chandelier, *60*
    Rustic Birch Candleholders, *95*
cardigan, Man's V-Neck, *126*-128
case, Traveling Slippers with, *129*-130
Catch a Falling Star, *14*-15
cedar, Sweet, Table Setting, *26*
centerpiece, 26, 29
    A Symphony in Silver, *94*
    By Candlelight, *94*
    Golden Angel, *32*-34

Golden Vines Wreath, *35*
Herb Garden, *30*-31
Holiday Pomanders, *92*
Poinsettia Basket, *21, 28*-29
Rustic Birch Candleholders, *95*
Sweet 'n Simple, *92*
chair, Pennsylvania Dutch Child's Rocking, *144*-147
chandelier, Christmas Kitchen, *60*
Checked Stocking, *62-63*, 66
church, Wooden, Ornament, 80, *83*
Cinnamon Stick Wreath, *10*
clothes, Bear, Rack, *148*, 152
Colonial Christmas Entryway Plaques, *11*
Color It Christmas Table Setting, *23*
cookie cutter
    Appliqués, *91*
    Ties, *90*-91
crèche, Balsa Wood Nativity Scene, *68*-71
Crepe Paper Flowers with Bows, *48*-49
cross stitch
    Country Mat, *42*
    "Happy Holidays," Table Runner, *43*-44
    Sampler Stocking, *62*-65

D

Dainty Mini-Stocking, *47*, 52-*53*
Dancing Santa Tree Topper, *78*-79
"Designer" Bath Towels, *103*
desk, The, Set, *103*
dinosaur, Pull-Along, *153*-154
doll
    Antique, Wreath, *3*-6
    Flower Girls, *139*-140

E

easy
    Evergreen Wreath, 11
    Mini-Wreaths, *96*-97
embroidery
    Fancy Cutwork Tablecloth, *36*-39
    Pineapple Afghan, *106*-107
entryway
    Colonial, Plaques, *11*
    Grand Entrance, 18-*19*
evergreen, Easy, Wreath, 11

F

Fancy Cutwork Tablecloth, *36*-39
Field of Flowers Wreath, *9*
flowers, 9, 29
    A Pretty Bowl of Posies, *51*
    Crepe Paper, with Bows, *48*-49
    Field of, Wreath, *9*
    Girls, *139*-140
    Ornaments, 23
Folk Art Goose, *7*-8
footstool, Pennsylvania Dutch, *108*-109
frame, Victorian Double, *119*-120
Frosty the Snowman & Jolly St. Nick Knitted Stockings, *62-63*, 66-67
furniture
    Pennsylvania Dutch Child's Rocking Chair, *144*-147
    Pennsylvania Dutch Footstool, *108*-109

G

garden, Herb, Centerpiece, *30*-31
Gifts of Nature Kissing Ball, *61*
girls, Flower, *139*-140
golden
    Angel, *32*-34
    Vines Wreath, *35*
goose, Folk Art, *7*-8
Grand Entrance, 18-*19*

H

"Happy Holidays" Cross Stitch Table Runner, *43*-44
Harvest Home Table Setting, *24*-25
hat, Winter Wonderland Sweaters &, *134*-136
Herald Angel Tree Topper, *86*-87
Herb Garden Centerpiece, *30*-31
holiday
    Hand Towel, *93*
    "Happy," Cross Stitch Table Runner, *43*-44
    Pomanders, *92*
    Simple Elegance, Table, *27*
Holly Bear Wreath, *12*-13
horse, Wooden, Ornament, 80-*81*

K

kitchen, Christmas Chandelier, *60*
knitting, 126
 Checked Stocking, *62-63*, 66
 Frosty the Snowman & Jolly St.
  Nick, Stockings, *62-63*, 66-67
 Man's V-Neck Cardigan, *126*-128
 Mitten Magic, *105, 137*-138
 Pineapple Afghan, *106*-107
 Sweetheart Sweater, *117*-118
 Winter Wonderland Sweaters &
  Hats, *134*-136
 Woman's Aran, Sweater, *114*-116

L

lace, Ruffles &, Layette, *141*, 143
lighting, 17-18
 Catch a Falling Star, *14*-15
 Grand Entrance, 18-*19*
 Rustic Tin Lanterns, *17*
locomotive, Sit-On, *155*, 154-157

M

magic, Mitten, *105, 137*-138
Man's V-Neck Cardigan, *126*-128
marquetry, Mountain Scene, Box,
 122-125
mat, Cross Stitch Country, *42*
Mitten Magic, *105, 137*-138
Mountain Scene Marquetry Box,
 122-125

N

napkin, 27
 Breakfast in Bed Tray &, Rings,
  98-99
 Christmas Morning Place
  Settings, *45*
 Winter Village Stenciled Tablecloth
  &, *40*-41
nativity, Balsa Wood, Scene, *68*-71
nature, Gifts of, Kissing Ball, *61*
needlepoint, Peek-a-Boo Santa, *74*-75

O

ornament
 Cookie Cutter Appliqués, *91*
 Crepe Paper Flowers with Bows,
  48-49
 Gifts of Nature Kissing Ball, *61*

Paper Santa, *72*-73
Peek-a-Boo Santa, *74*-75
Peppermint-Striped, *57*
Santa Sack, *76*-77
Secret Santa, *76*-77
Wooden Wonderland, *80*-85
O Tannenbaum Tree Skirt, *58*-59

P

paper
 Crepe, Flowers with Bows, *48*-49
 Santa Ornament, *72*-73
patchwork, Ribbon, Stocking, *62*-64
Peek-a-Boo Santa, *74*-75
pennsylvania
 Dutch Child's Rocking Chair, *144*-
  147
 Dutch Footstool, *108*-109
Peppermint-Striped Ornaments, *57*
pillow, Ruffles & Lace, *141*, 143
Pineapple Afghan, *106*-107
plaque
 Colonial Christmas Entryway, *11*
 Folk Art Goose, *7*-8
poinsettia, Basket, *21, 28*-29
pomander, Holiday, *92*
posies, A Pretty Bowl of, *51*
Potato-Stamp Wrap, 133
potpourri, 101
 Holiday Pomanders, *92*
 Sweet Sachets, *100*-101
Pull-Along Dinosaur, *153*-154
Puppy Palace, *110*-113
puzzle, Bear Family, *148*, 150-151

Q

Quick Tile Trivet, 99
quilting
 O Tannenbaum Tree Skirt, *58*-59
 Ruffles & Lace, *141*, 143
 White, Stocking, *62*-64

R

rabbit, Velveteen, 54, *55*
rack
 Bear Clothes, *148*, 152
 Toiletries, *131*-132
Ribbon Patchwork Stocking, *62*-64
rocking chair, Pennsylvania Dutch
 Child's, *144*-147

Ruffles & Lace Layette, *141*, 143
rustic
 Birch Candleholders, *95*
 Tin Lanterns, *17*

S

sachet, Sweet, *100*-101
sack, Santa, *76*-77
sacque, Buttercup Baby, *141*, 140-143
Sampler Stocking, *62*-65
santa
 Dancing, Tree Topper, *78*-79
 Frosty the Snowman & Jolly St. Nick
  Knitted Stockings, *62-63*, 66-67
 Paper, Ornament, *72*-73
 Peek-a-Boo, *74*-75
 Sack, *76*-77
 Secret, *76*-77
 Stocking, *76*-77
Secret Santa, *76*-77
Shower Shelf, *131*, 133
silver, A Symphony in, *94*
Simple Elegance Holiday Table, *27*
Sit-On Locomotive, *155*, 154-157
slippers, Traveling, with Case,
 129-130
snowman, Frosty the, & Jolly St. Nick
 Knitted Stockings, *62-63*, 66-67
soldier, Wooden, with Trumpet
 Ornament, 80, *84*-85
star, Catch a Falling, *14*-15
stencil
 O Tannenbaum Tree Skirt, *58*-59
 Winter Village, Tablecloth &
  Napkins, *40*-41
St. Nick, Frosty the Snowman and
 Jolly, Knitted Stockings, *62-63*,
  66-67
stocking
 Checked, *62-63*, 66
 Dainty Mini-, *47*, 52-53
 Frosty the Snowman & Jolly St. Nick
  Knitted, *62-63*, 66-67
 Ribbon Patchwork, *62*-64
 Sampler, *62*-65
 Santa, *76*-77
 Victorian Velvet, *54*-55
 White Quilted, *62*-64
sweater
 Man's V-Neck Cardigan, *126*-128
 Sweetheart, *117*-118
 Winter Wonderland, & Hats, *134*-136
 Woman's Aran Knit, *114*-116

sweet
  'n Simple, *92*
  Cedar Table Setting, *26*
  Sachets, *100*-101
Sweetheart Sweater, *117*-118
symphony, A, in Silver, *94*

T

tablecloth
  Fancy Cutwork, *36*-39
  Winter Village Stenciled, & Napkins,
    40-41
table runner, "Happy Holidays" Cross
  Stitch, *43*-44
table setting
  Color It Christmas, *23*
  Harvest Home, *24*-25
  Simple elegance Holiday, *27*
  Sweet Cedar, *26*
  Victorian Sparkle, *22*-23
Take a Note! Book, *89*, 102
Teddy Pull Toy, *148*-150
The Bear Necessities, *148*-152
The Desk Set, *103*
tile, Quick, Trivet, 99
tin, Rustic, Lanterns, *17*
Toiletries Rack, *131*-132

towel
  "Designer" Bath, *103*
  Holiday Hand, *93*
toy
  Bear Family Puzzles, *148*, 150-151
  Flower Girls, *139*-140
  Pull-Along Dinosaur, *153*-154
  Sit-On Locomotive, *155*, 154-157
  Teddy-Pull, *148*-152
  Velveteen Rabbits, 54, *55*
Traveling Slippers with Case, *129*-130
tray, Breakfast in Bed, & Napkin Rings,
  98-99
tree skirt, O Tannenbaum, *58*-59
tree topper
  Dancing Santa, *78*-79
  Herald Angel, *86*-87
trivet, Quick Tile, 99

 V

Velveteen Rabbits, 54
victorian
  Double Frame, *119*-120
  Sparkle Table Setting, *22*-23
  Velvet Stockings, *54*-55
Victoriana Wreath, *50*
village
  Winter, Window Scene, *16*

Winter, Stenciled Tablecloth &
  Napkins, *40*-41
vines, Golden, Wreath, *35*

 W

window, Winter Village, Scene, *16*
White Quilted Stocking, *62*-64
winter
  Village Stenciled Tablecloth &
    Napkins, *40*-41
  Village Window Scene, *16*
  Wonderland Sweaters & Hats,
    134-136
Woman's Aran Knit Sweater, *114*-116
Wooden Wonderland Ornaments,
  80-85
wreath, 11
  Antique Doll, *3*-6
  Christmas Kitchen Chandelier, *60*
  Cinnamon Stick, *10*
  Cookie Cutter Ties, *90*-91
  Easy Evergreen, 11
  Easy Mini-, *96*-97
  Field of Flowers, *9*
  Golden Vines, *35*
  Holly Bear, *12*-13
  Victoriana, *50*

PHOTOGRAPHERS

Robert Ander: *Page 92*. David Bishop: *Pages 7, 27, 28, 36, 42, 43*. Richard Blinkoff: *Pages 129, 131*.
Leombruno Bodi: *Page 106*. Ralph Bogertman: *Pages 9, 11, 16, 19, 22, 26, 93*. Richard Cappellutti: *Pages 78,
139*. David Glomb: *Pages 21, 23*. Joseph Heppt: *Pages 129, 131, 144, 153*. Elyse Lewin: *Pages 56, 57*. Taylor Lewis:
Pages 10, 17, 92, 94. Bill McGinn: *Pages 12, 30-31, 32, 40, 58, 60, 62-63, 72, 74, 80, 81, 82, 83, 84 89, 94, 95, 102,
105, 108, 110, 119, 120, 129, 131, 134, 137, 144, 148, 153, 155*. Ron Nicolayen: *Page 114*. Jeff Niki: *Pages 117,
122, 126, 141*. Bradley Olman: *Page 10*. Frances Pellegrini: *Pages 3, 4, 24-25, 48, 50, 51, 100*. Dean Powell: *Pages
35, 45, 61, 96-97*. Ron Schwerin: *Pages 180, 204*. Michael Skott: *Page 162*. Gordon E. Smith: *Pages 14,
172*. Michael Soluri: *Pages 47, 53*. Bob Stoller: *Pages 90, 91, 103*. Rene Velez: *Pages 10, 12, 32, 40, 58, 62-63, 68-
69, 72, 74, 77, 80, 81, 82, 83, 84, 86, 95, 103, 105, 108, 110, 119, 120, 129, 131, 134, 137, 139, 144, 148, 153,
155*. Elizabeth Zeschin: *Page 55*.

CONTRIBUTING CRAFT EDITORS

Pam Aulson: *Pages 90, 91*. Joanne Beretta: *Pages 14, 30-31*. Michael Cannarozzi: *Page 72*. Marci Crestani: *Pages 21,
23, 28*. Alexandra Eames: *Pages 16, 19*. Bonnie Egli: *Page 74*. Vicki Enteen: *Pages 62-63*. Wendy Everett: *Page
141*. Blake Hampton: *Pages 68-69, 78, 80, 81, 82, 83, 84, 86*. Sang Han: *Page 119*. Priscilla Hauser: *Page
108*. Margot Hotchkiss: *Pages 35, 55, 61, 96-97*. Alla Ladyzhensky: *Pages 42, 43, 62-63*. Eleanor Lewis: *Pages 30-
31*. Steve Levine: *Page 122*. Patricia Marks: *Page 106*. Buff McAllister: *Page 153*. Cathy Miller: *Page 10*. Jill Morris:
Page 139. Josephine Neri: *Page 120*. Niddy Noddy: *Page 126*. Kathy Orr: *Pages 47, 53*. Lillian Pacelli: *Page
32*. Audrey Peyton: *Page 134*. Robert Pfreundschuh: *Page 95*. Mary Jane Protus (for Paton Yarns): *Page 117*.
Evelyn Rodriguez: *Page 141*. Barbara Schultz: *Page 7*. Jane Slovachek: *Pages 62-63, 105, 137*. Michelle Slovak:
Pages 60, 94. Tom Tavernor: *Page 110*. Jean Wilkinson: *Pages 48, 50, 51*. Doris Wright: *Pages 62-63*. Joanne Young:
Page 92.